Oxford SKILLS WORLD

Listening 3

with Speaking

Jill Korey O'Sullivan

OXFORD
UNIVERSITY PRESS

OXFORD
UNIVERSITY PRESS

198 Madison Avenue
New York, NY 10016 USA
Great Clarendon Street, Oxford, OX2 6DP, United Kingdom

Oxford University Press is a department of the University of Oxford.
It furthers the University's objective of excellence in research, scholarship,
and education by publishing worldwide. Oxford is a registered trade
mark of Oxford University Press in the UK and in certain other countries

ISBN: 978 0 19 411338 0 STUDENT BOOK WITH WORKBOOK

Printed in China

This book is printed on paper from certified and well-managed sources

ACKNOWLEDGMENTS

Cover illustration and main character illustrations by: Shane McGowan/The
Organisation
Cover photograph: Johner Images/Getty
Back cover photograph: Oxford University Press building/David Fisher

Student Book

Illustrations by: Robin Boyer/Illustration Online pp.11, 36, 46, 68–69; Mattia
Cerato/MB Artists pp.8–9, 72; Monique Dong/Bright Group pp.22–23, 82–83;
Kevin Fales/Maggie Byers Sprinzeles pp.18, 57, 78–79, 81; Chris Jones/Maggie
Byers Sprinzeles pp.32, 41B, 43, 58, 88; Margeaux Lucas/MB Artists pp.26–27,
29, 71; Juan Moreno/MB Artists pp.40B, 41A, 65, 67; Susanna Rumiz/Lemonade
Illustration pp.37, 39, 54–55; Christos Skaltsas/Advocate Art pp.15, 25, 50;
Jomike Tejido/MB Artists pp.12, 64, 85–86; Laura Watson/Illustration Online
pp.30, 51, 53

*The Publishers would like to thank the following for their kind permission to reproduce
photographs and other copyright material:* 123rf: pp.16 (cashier/Dmitry
Kalinovsky), 40 (thick book/Dmitriy Moroz); Alamy: pp.22 (calculator/chris
brignell), 26 (drawer/SOURCENEXT), 28 (drawer/SOURCENEXT), 42 (dirty
pants/Desintegrator), 64 (music lesson/GoGo Images Corporation), (watching
a play/zixia), 68 (children walking/Hero Images), 70 (4a/Hero Images);
Getty: pp.8 (judge/DarrenMower), (tailor/SeanShot), 12 (author/Chicasso),
13 (firefighter/DarthArt), 14 (author/Chicasso), 20–21 (children in classroom/
Hero Images), 26 (cabinet/pbombaert), (flag/Thinkstock), 28 (cabinet/
pbombaert), 50 (airport/AmandaLewis), (bank/YinYang), 52 (mailboxes/
RiverNorthPhotography), 64 (child swimming/Elisabeth Schmitt), (art class/
mediaphotos), (child writing email/Sidekick), 66 (audience watching play/
Caiaimage/Robert Daly), (boy on laptop/Jose Luis Pelaez Inc.), (boy painting/
FatCamera), 68 (children having fun/kali9), (girl making model/Donald Iain
Smith), 70 (1a/KidStock), (1b/Bec Parsons), (3a/kali9), (4b/Donald Iain Smith),
78 (stairs/Richard Hylerstedt/EyeEm); Oxford University Press: pp.10 (scientist/
Shutterstock/A and N photography), (reporter/Shutterstock/michaeljung),
12 (astronaut/Shutterstock/NikoNomad), (engineer/Shutterstock;
anyaivanova), 14 (astronaut/Shutterstock/NikoNomad), (mechanic/123rf/Luca
Bertolli), 22 (dictionary/MM Studios), (scissors/Shutterstock; BonD80), (stapler/
Shutterstock/Naruedom Yaempongsa), 24 (scissors/Oxford University Press
ANZ), (calculator/Shutterstock/Sura Nualpradid), 26 (laptop/Shutterstock; Vtls),
(tablet/Shutterstock; Thaiview), 28 (laptop/Shutterstock; Vtls), (tablet/123rf),
36 (shorts/Gareth Boden), 38 (handbag/Shutterstock/Karkas), 40 (clean shoes/
Shutterstock/Cesarz), 42 (thick coat/Shutterstock/Polryaz), (clean shoes/
Shutterstock/Cesarz), 50 (post office/), 52 (airport/Shutterstock/Rawpixel.
com), 54 (amusement park/Shutterstock), (apartment/Shutterstock; Ralf
Gosch), (restaurant/Shutterstock/Monkey Business Images), 56 (amusement
park in day/Shutterstock), (restaurant/Shutterstock/Monkey Business Images),
(amusement park at night/Shutterstock), 60 (asking directions/Chris King),
62–63 (children in music class/Shutterstock/Monkey Business Images),
78 (brush/Shutterstock/Singhanart), (garden/Shutterstock; SGM), 80 (comb/
Shutterstock/You Touch Pix of EuToch), 82 (rug/Shutterstock; Africa Studio),
84 (4b/Shutterstock; Africa Studio); Shutterstock: pp.6–7 (construction
workers/potowizard), 8 (taxi driver/Diego Cervo), (musician/Sergei Butorin),
(news reporter/michaeljung), (scientist/Gorodenkoff), 10 (judge/sirtravelalot),
(taxi driver/Africa Studio), 12 (cashier/Odua Images), (mechanic/ESB
Professional), (singer/SFROLOV), 13 (mechanic/wavebreakmedia), 14 (engineer/
Monkey Business Images), (cashier/michaeljung), (singer/SFROLOV), (author/
ArtFamily), (astronaut/Bakhur Nick), 16 (astronaut/Dotted Yeti), (tailor/
UfaBizPhoto), 22 (folder/photastic), 24 (stapler/Stockforlife), 26 (shelf/
donatas1205), 28 (open drawer/Africa Studio), (shelf/donatas1205), (cabinet/
Stokkete), (South Korean flag/ayzek), 34–35 (teenage girls shopping/Syda
Productions), 36 (baseball cap/Etaphop photo), (coat/Karkas), (handbag/
Daniel Heighton), (sneakers/Beyla Balla), (swimsuit/Ruslan Kudrin), 38 (coat/
ludmilafoto), (swimsuit/Michael Kraus), (sneakers/yoshi0511), 40 (dirty shoes/
Malota), (heavy weight/SS1001), (light weight/FabrikaSimf), (thin book/
Annado), 42 (clean pants/Karkas), (light weight/FabrikaSimf), (heavy weight/
SS1001), (think coat/gogoiso), (dirty shoes/Malota), 44 (firefighter's uniform/
Flashon Studio), (baseball player's uniform/3DMI), (basketball players uniform/
Prostock-studio), 48–49 (crowded subway platform/Aleksandar Todorovic),
50 (home/Luis Santos), (playground/Jack schiffer), (zoo/txking), 52 (playground/
Glynsimages2013), (house/ppa), 54 (bookstore/Radu Bercan), (museum/Gimas),
(school/s4svisuals), 56 (school exterior/Piotr Wawrzyniuk), (bookstore/Radu
Bercan), (museum/MarKord), (apartment/LJB33), (school interior/s4svisuals),
64 (violin practice/Monkey Business Images), 66 (girl playing violin/Blend
Images), 68 (boy listening to music/Syda Productions), (children playing
board game/wavebreakmedia), (boy taking a nap/Karen Grigoryan), 70 (2a/
Syda Productions), (2b/Africa Studio), (3b/Chubykin Arkady), 74 (boy making
model/AVAVA), 76–77 (Mongolian yurts/withGod), 78 (comb/R3BV), (mirror/
outc), (sink/iiiphevgeniy), 80 (sink/Torsak Thammachote), (garden/fotocraft),
(mirror/lttidech), 82 (armchair/kibri_ho), (bathtub/3DMI), (oven/Pro3DArtt),
(refridgerator/Pro3DArtt), (sofa/Pix11), 84 (1a/Pro3DArtt), (1b/kibri_ho), (2a/
Pix11), (2b/LifetimeStock), (3a/Pro3DArtt), (3b/Africa Studio), (4a/Pro3DArtt)

Workbook

Illustrations by: Mattia Cerato/MB Artists pp.111, 113; Monique Dong/Bright
Group p.101; Chris Jones/Maggie Byers Sprinzeles p.105; Margeaux Lucas/
MB Artists p.97; Juan Moreno/MB Artists p.91; Christos Skaltsas/Advocate Art
p.109; Jomike Tejido/MB Artists pp.93, 103; Laura Watson/Illustration Online
p.107

*The Publishers would like to thank the following for their kind permission to
reproduce photographs and other copyright material:* 123rf: p.102 (1c/Dmitriy
Moroz); Alamy: pp.95 (stapler/Axpitel), 98 (3c/SOURCENEXT), 99 (1890s
clothing/Aleksandr Kichigin), 102 (3a/Desintegrator), 108 (1a/GoGo Images
Corporation), (3b/zixia), 110 (1a/Hero Images); Getty: pp.92 (1a/SeanShot),
(2b/DarrenMower), 94 (1b/Chicasso), 98 (3a/pbombaert), 99 (1980s clothing/
izusek), 104 (3a/AmandaLewis), (3b/YinYang), 108 (1b/Caiaimage/Robert
Daly), (2a/Sidekick), (2b/Elisabeth Schmitt), (3a/mediaphotos), (4a/Jose Luis
Pelaez Inc.), 110 (2c/Donald Iain Smith), (3a/KidStock), (3c/kali9), 112 (1a/
Richard Hylerstedt/EyeEm); Oxford University Press: pp.92 (4a/Shutterstock/A
and N photography), 94 (1a/anyaivanova), (2c/123rf/Luca Bertolli), (3a/
NikoNomad), (3b/anyaivanova), 96 (1a/Naruedom Yaempongsa), (1b/MM
Studios), (3a/Shutterstock; BonD80), (3b/Shutterstock/Sura Nualpradid), (4a/
Oxford University Press ANZ), 98 (1b/Vtls), (1c/123rf), 100 (2b/Karkas), (3b/
Gareth Boden), 102 (2a/Shutterstock/Cesarz), (3c/Gareth Boden), 104 (1b/),
(2a/Shutterstock/Rawpixel.com), 106 (1a/Shutterstock; Ralf Gosch), (1c/
Shutterstock), (3a/Shutterstock), (3c/Shutterstock/Monkey Business Images),
112 (2a/Shutterstock; SGM), (2b/Shutterstock/Singhanart), (4b/Shutterstock/
You Touch Pix of EuToch), 114 (2b/Shutterstock; Africa Studio); Shutterstock:
pp.92 (1b/Gorodenkoff), (2a/Sergei Butorin), (3a/michaeljung), (3b/
sirtravelalot), (4b/Diego Cervo), 94 (1c/ESB Professional), (2a/Odua Images), (2b/
Bakhur Nick), (3c/michaeljung), 95 (abacus/Kokliang), 96 (2a/photastic), (4b/
Stockforlife), 98 (1a/Stokkete), (2a/Dja65), (2b/Thaiview), (2c/donatas1205), (3b/
donatas1205), 100 (1a/Etaphop photo), (1b/yoshi0511), (2a/Karkas), (3a/Michael
Kraus), (4a/Beyla Balla), (4b/Daniel Heighton), 102 (1a/Annado), (1b/Nataliass),
(2b/yoshi0511), (2c/Malota), (3b/Karkas), 104 (1a/Jack schiffer), (2b/Luis Santos),
(4a/Glynsimages2013), (4b/txking), 106 (1b/Piotr Wawrzyniuk), (2a/Gimas), (2b/
s4svisuals), (2c/Radu Bercan), (3b/MarKord), 108 (4b/Blend Images), 110 (1b/
Karen Grigoryan), (1c/Syda Productions), (2a/wavebreakmedia), (2b/Africa
Studio), (3b/Syda Productions), 112 (1b/outc), (3a/iiiphevgeniy), (3b/R3BV), (4a/
fotocraft), 114 (1a/3DMI), (1b/Pro3DArtt), (1c/Pro3DArtt), (2a/kibri_ho), (2c/
Pix11), (3a/Africa Studio), (3b/LifetimeStock), (3c/Pro3DArtt)

Table of Contents

Hi! I'm Olly.

Hi, I'm Molly!

Introduction

Welcome to Oxford Skills World

Oxford Skills World: Listening with Speaking is a flexible paired skills course that takes students on a journey toward independent learning, providing them with strategies and support to reach their goals.

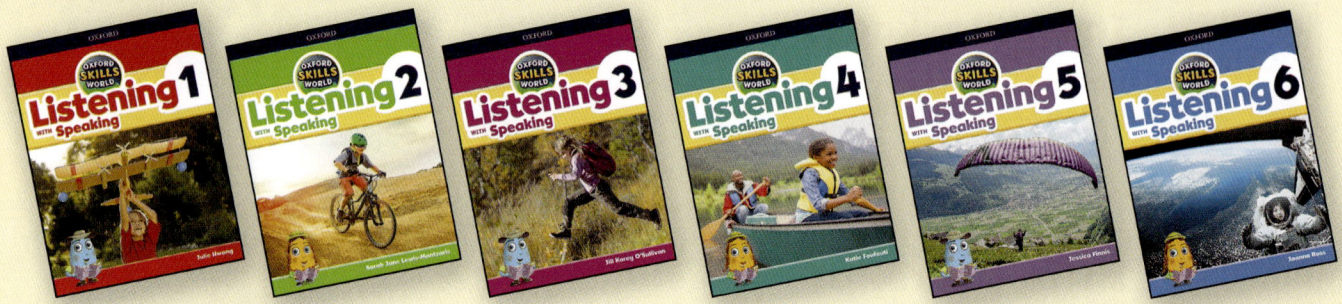

For Students

- Student Book / Workbook
- Student's website with downloadable audio and extra resources
  www.oup.com/elt/oxfordskillsworld

For Teachers

- Downloadable Teacher's Pack with instructional support, assessment, professional development videos, projects, and speaking resources
- Classroom Presentation Tool
- Teacher's website with downloadable audio and extra resources
  www.oup.com/elt/teacher/oxfordskillsworld

Be the Leader on Your Skills Adventure!

Hi! We're Olly and Molly, your skills adventure guides. We help you reach your goals by introducing new listening and speaking strategies, asking helpful questions, and giving friendly reminders. Most importantly, we cheer you on every step of the way! Let's go!

Quick Guide

Inside Each Topic

Topic Opener

Theme-based topics provide high-interest content relevant to students' lives.

My Goals introduces students to the objectives of each unit in the topic.*

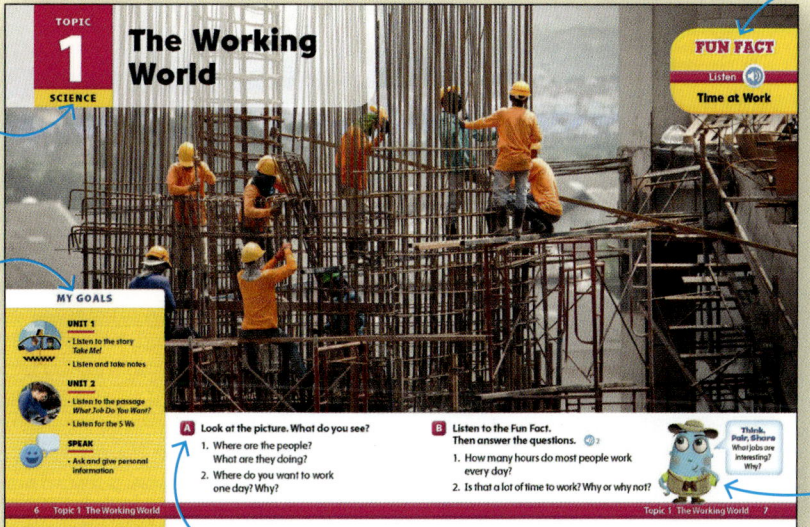

Students listen to a Fun Fact to increase their engagement with the topic.

Fun characters, Olly and Molly, encourage 21st century skills like critical thinking, collaboration, and communication.

Students answer questions to activate prior knowledge and think critically.

Get Ready to Listen • Listen

Students learn and practice new vocabulary and complete the picture dictionary at the back of the book.

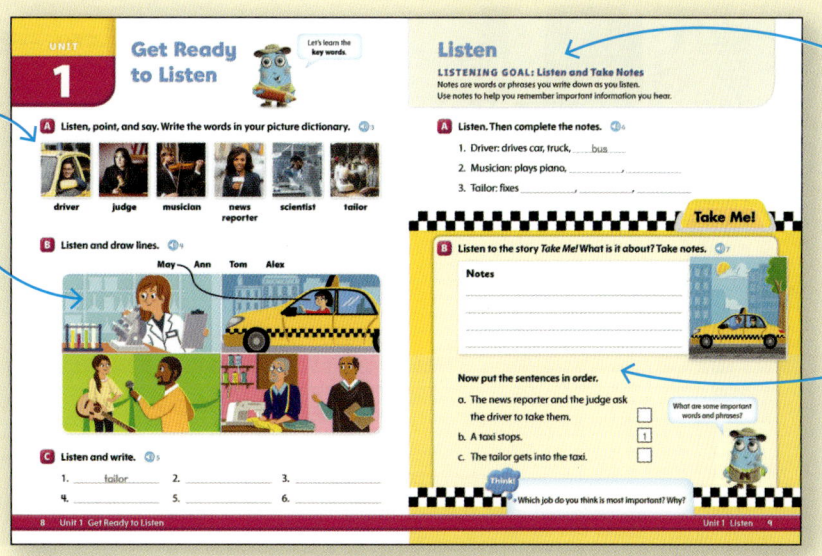

Listening Goals are strategies students can apply to any passage.

Students apply strategies to high-interest fiction and nonfiction passages, think critically about what they hear, and make connections to their own lives.

*Each topic contains two thematically related units.

Quick Guide

Understand

Students increase their comprehension of the passages by applying listening strategies they have learned.

Students complete activities to strengthen their understanding of the unit's vocabulary.

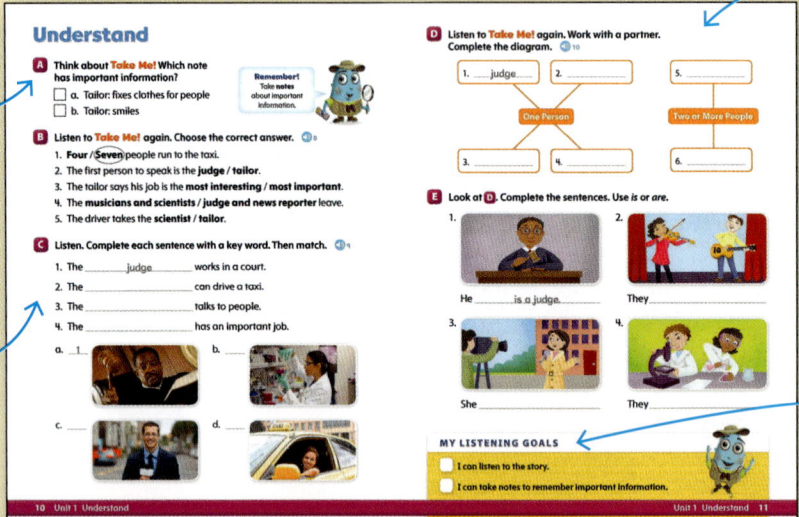

Students demonstrate comprehension of the unit's passage, vocabulary, and grammar.

At the end of each unit, students assess the progress they have made toward achieving their goals.

Listening Check

With helpful reminders from Olly and Molly, students apply the **Listening Goals** from both units to a new text.

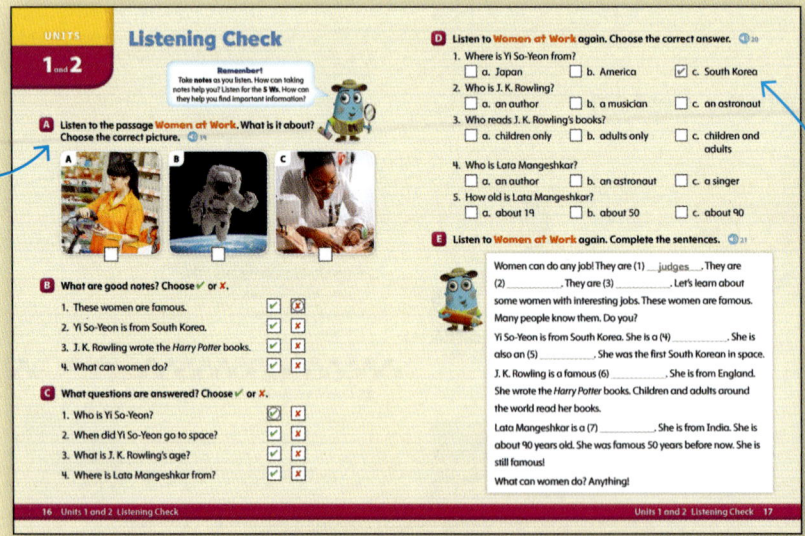

Students complete activities to boost listening comprehension and vocabulary application.

Get Ready to Speak • Speak

Speaking Goals prepare students to speak in different contexts.

Speaking Tips provide guidance on grammar, punctuation, and mechanics and help students speak fluently and accurately.

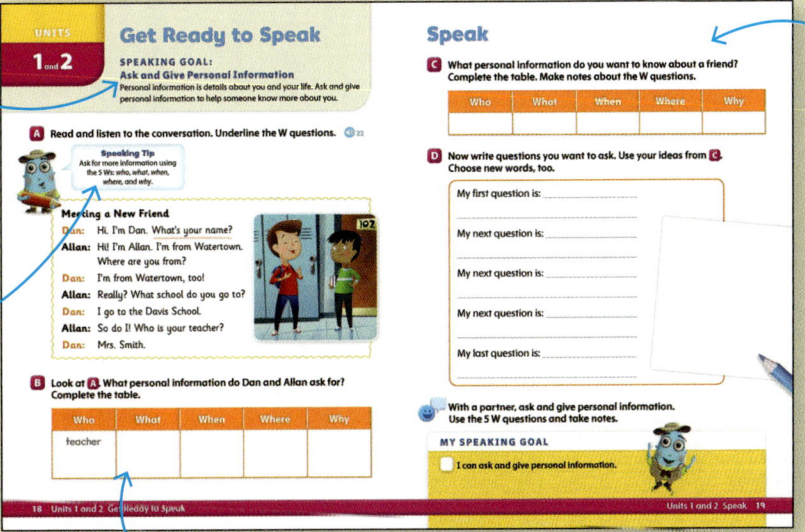

Scaffolded speaking models help students accomplish their speaking goals.

Students use graphic organizers to comprehend speaking models and to organize their thoughts for their own speaking.

Workbook

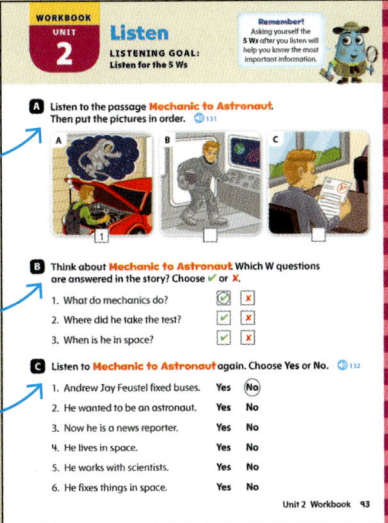

Workbook pages at the end of the book provide more opportunities for students to apply their **Listening Goals** and boost comprehension.

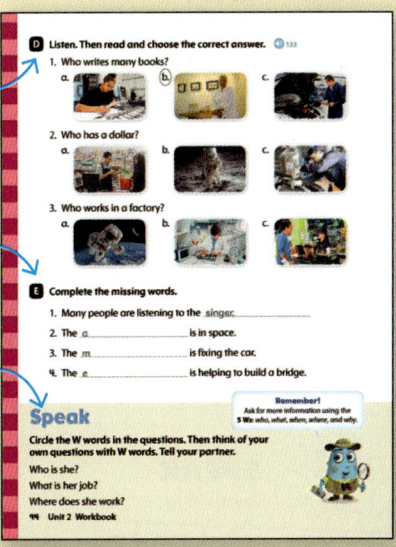

Additional activities provide extra opportunities for listening comprehension and vocabulary practice.

Students apply the topic's **Speaking Tip** to ensure proper usage in their own speaking.

TOPIC

1

SCIENCE

The Working World

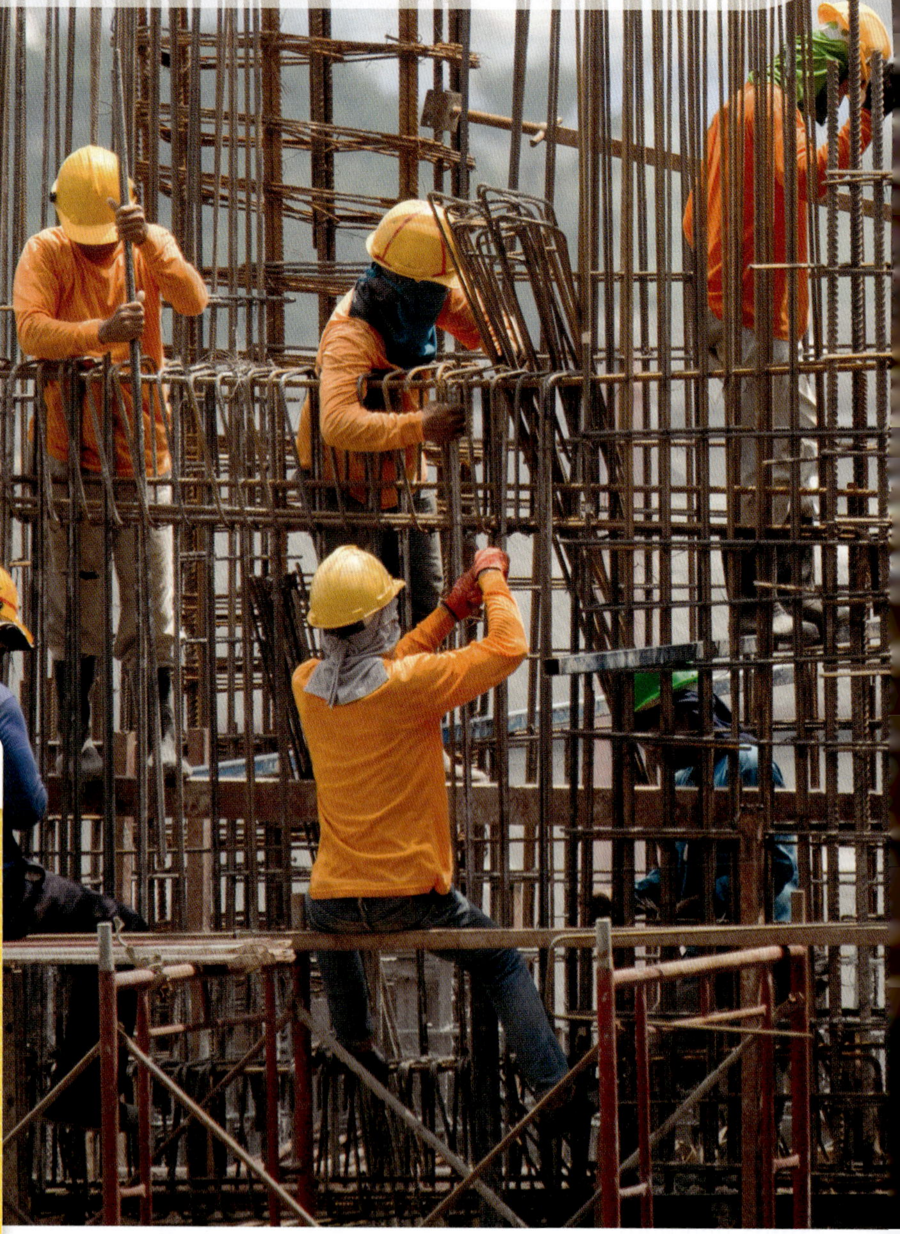

MY GOALS

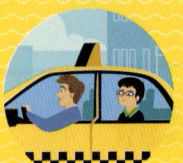

UNIT 1

- Listen to the story *Take Me!*
- Listen and take notes

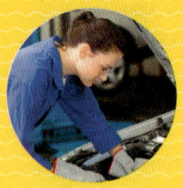

UNIT 2

- Listen to the passage *What Job Do You Want?*
- Listen for the 5 Ws

SPEAK

- Ask and give personal information

A **Look at the picture. What do you see?**

1. Where are the people? What are they doing?
2. Where do you want to work one day? Why?

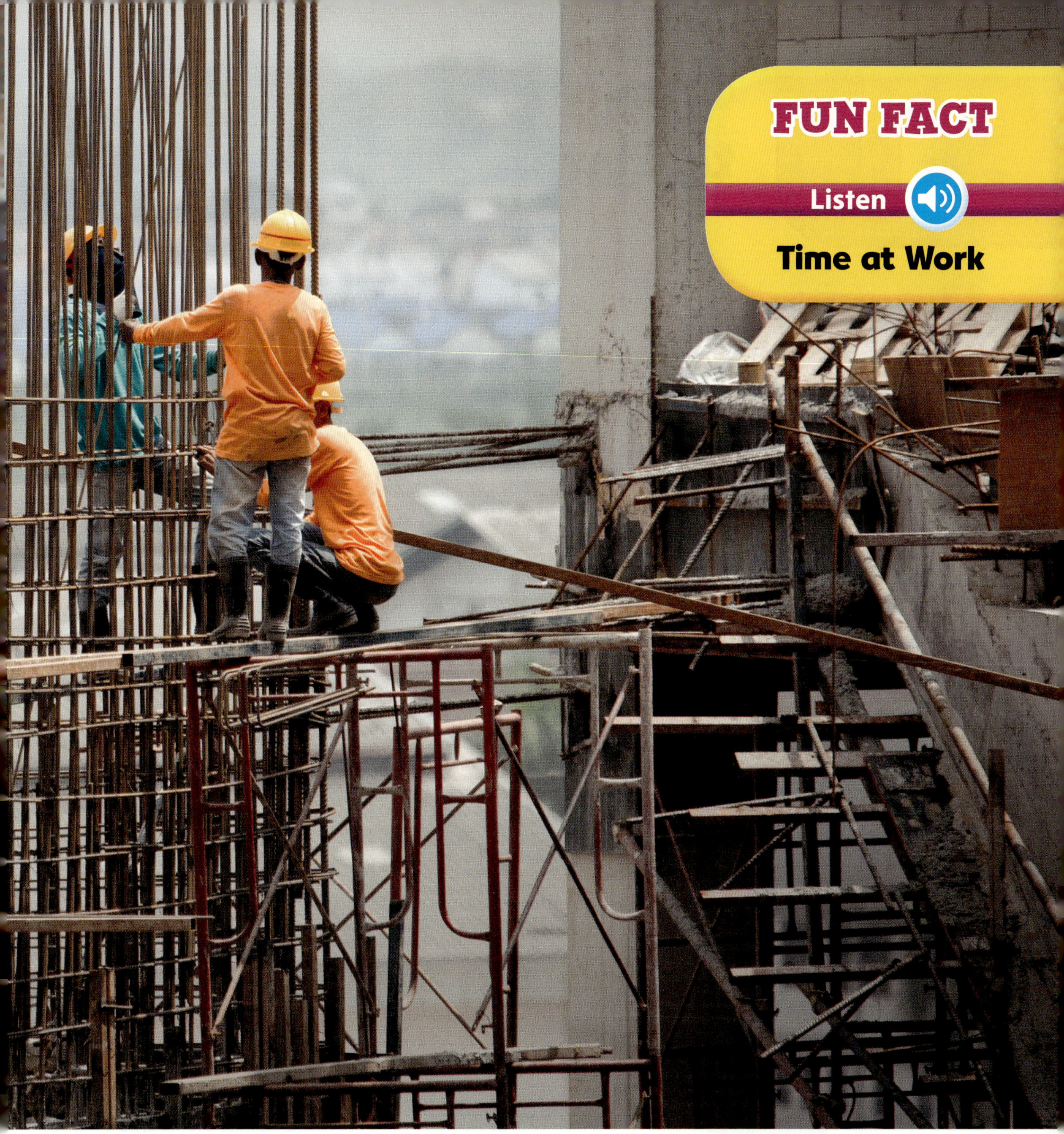

Listen

Time at Work

B Listen to the Fun Fact.
Then answer the questions. 🔊 2

1. How many hours do most people work
   every day?

2. Is that a lot of time to work? Why or why not?

**Think,
Pair, Share**
What jobs are
interesting?
Why?

Get Ready to Listen

Let's learn the **key words**.

A Listen, point, and say. Write the words in your picture dictionary. 3

driver   **judge**   **musician**   **news reporter**   **scientist**   **tailor**

B Listen and draw lines. 4

May   Ann   Tom   Alex

C Listen and write. 5

1.  tailor   2. _____   3. _____

4. _____   5. _____   6. _____

Listen

LISTENING GOAL: Listen and Take Notes

Notes are words or phrases you write down as you listen.
Use notes to help you remember important information you hear.

A **Listen. Then complete the notes.** 🔊 6

1. Driver: drives car, truck, _____bus_____

2. Musician: plays piano, _____, _____

3. Tailor: fixes _____, _____, _____

Take Me!

B **Listen to the story _Take Me!_ What is it about? Take notes.** 🔊 7

Notes

_____

_____

_____

_____

Now put the sentences in order.

a. The news reporter and the judge ask the driver to take them. ☐

b. A taxi stops. 1

c. The tailor gets into the taxi. ☐

What are some important words and phrases?

Think!

• Which job do you think is most important? Why?

Understand

A **Think about Take Me!** Which note has important information?

☐ a. Tailor: fixes clothes for people

☐ b. Tailor: smiles

> **Remember!**
> Take **notes** about important information.

B Listen to **Take Me!** again. Choose the correct answer. 🔊 8

1. **Four** / **Seven** people run to the taxi.

2. The first person to speak is the **judge** / **tailor**.

3. The tailor says his job is the **most interesting** / **most important**.

4. The **musicians and scientists** / **judge and news reporter** leave.

5. The driver takes the **scientist** / **tailor**.

C Listen. Complete each sentence with a key word. Then match. 🔊 9

1. The _____judge_____ works in a court.

2. The _____ can drive a taxi.

3. The _____ talks to people.

4. The _____ has an important job.

a. __1__

b. ____

c. ____

d. ____

D Listen to **Take Me!** again. Work with a partner. Complete the diagram. 🔊 10

1. ___judge___

2. _____

5. _____

One Person

Two or More People

3. _____

4. _____

6. _____

E Look at **D**. Complete the sentences. Use *is* or *are*.

1.

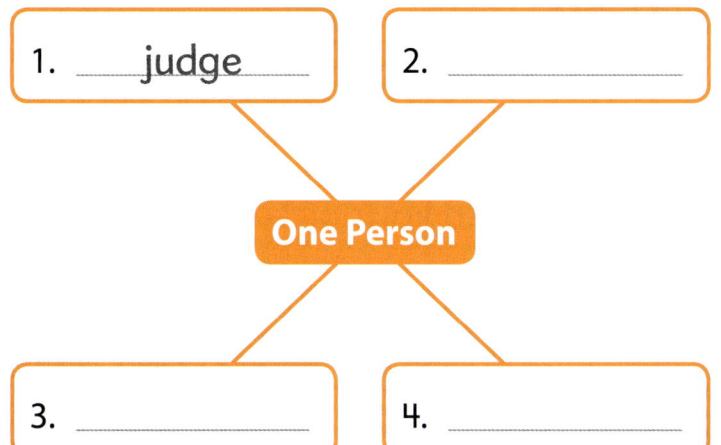

He _____ is a judge. _____

2.

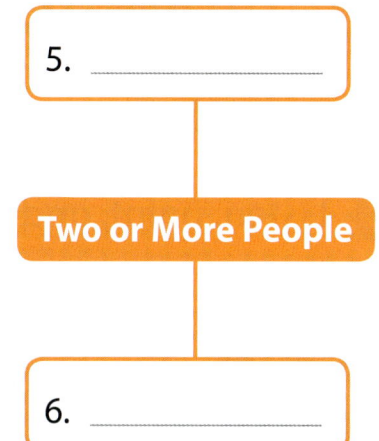

They _____

3.

She _____

4.

They _____

MY LISTENING GOALS

☐ I can listen to the story.

☐ I can take notes to remember important information.

Get Ready to Listen

Let's learn the **key words**.

A Listen, point, and say. Write the words in your picture dictionary. 11

| astronaut | author | cashier | engineer | mechanic | singer |

B Listen and number. 12

C Listen and complete the sentences. 13

1. The _____cashier_____ works eight hours every day.

2. The _____ and the _____ are fixing the problem together.

3. The _____ has an exciting job.

4. The _____ and the _____ are friends.

Listen

LISTENING GOAL: Listen for the 5 Ws
The 5 Ws are *who, what, when, where,* and *why.* After you listen,
ask yourself the 5 Ws to know the most important information.

A Listen. What does the sentence tell you? 14

1. ☐ a. why   ☑ b. where
2. ☐ a. what   ☐ b. when
3. ☐ a. when   ☐ b. where

---

www.jobcorner.osw/whatjobdoyouwant

What Job Do You Want?

B Listen to the passage *What Job Do You Want?*
What is it about? Choose the correct picture. 15

A ☐

B ☐

Now choose ✔ or ✘.

1. The people are talking in a classroom. ✔ ✘
2. The people are talking about their jobs. ✔ ✘
3. One person is a cashier. ✔ ✘

> What information
> do you learn
> about each job?

Think!
• Which job is interesting to you? Why?

Understand

A Think about **What Job Do You Want?**
Did you hear the answers to these questions?
Choose **Yes** or **No**.

1. What does an engineer do? **Yes** **No**
2. Where do authors work? **Yes** **No**

Remember!
When you listen, the **5 Ws**
(*who, what, when, where, why*) help you know the
most important information.

B Listen to **What Job Do You Want?** again.
Choose the correct answer. 🔊 16

1. Where do mechanics work?
   - ☑ a. garages
   - ☐ b. schools
2. Who is an engineer?
   - ☐ a. Bill
   - ☐ b. Jan
3. What is Ellen's job?
   - ☐ a. She's an engineer.
   - ☐ b. She's an astronaut.

C Listen and choose the correct picture. Then write the key word. 🔊 17

1.
- ☑ a.
- ☐ b.

2.
- ☐ a.
- ☐ b.

engineer

3.
- ☐ a.
- ☐ b.

4.
- ☐ a.
- ☐ b.

D Listen to **What Job Do You Want?** again. Work with a partner. Complete the table. 🔊 18

What do …	What does …
1. mechanics	2.
3.	4.

E Look at **D**. Write. Ask about the job. Use *What* + *do* or *does*.

1.

What do mechanics do?

2.

3.

4.

Listening Check

A Listen to the passage **Women at Work**. What is it about? Choose the correct picture. 🔊 19

A

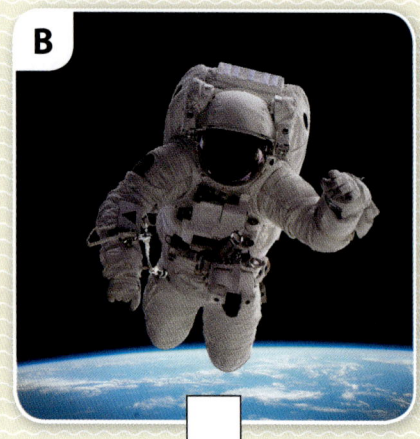

B

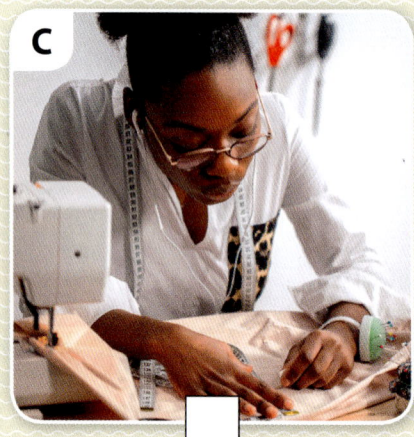

C

B What are good notes? Choose ✔ or ✘.

1. These women are famous. ✔ ⊗

2. Yi So-Yeon is from South Korea. ✔ ✘

3. J. K. Rowling wrote the *Harry Potter* books. ✔ ✘

4. What can women do? ✔ ✘

C What questions are answered? Choose ✔ or ✘.

1. Who is Yi So-Yeon? ✅ ✘

2. When did Yi So-Yeon go to space? ✔ ✘

3. What is J. K. Rowling's age? ✔ ✘

4. Where is Lata Mangeshkar from? ✔ ✘

D Listen to **Women at Work** again. Choose the correct answer. 🔊 20

1. Where is Yi So-Yeon from?
   ☐ a. Japan ☐ b. America ☑ c. South Korea

2. Who is J. K. Rowling?
   ☐ a. an author ☐ b. a musician ☐ c. an astronaut

3. Who reads J. K. Rowling's books?
   ☐ a. children only ☐ b. adults only ☐ c. children and adults

4. Who is Lata Mangeshkar?
   ☐ a. an author ☐ b. an astronaut ☐ c. a singer

5. How old is Lata Mangeshkar?
   ☐ a. about 19 ☐ b. about 50 ☐ c. about 90

E Listen to **Women at Work** again. Complete the sentences. 🔊 21

Women can do any job! They are (1) __judges__ . They are (2) _____ . They are (3) _____ . Let's learn about some women with interesting jobs. These women are famous. Many people know them. Do you?

Yi So-Yeon is from South Korea. She is a (4) _____ . She is also an (5) _____ . She was the first South Korean in space.

J. K. Rowling is a famous (6) _____ . She is from England. She wrote the *Harry Potter* books. Children and adults around the world read her books.

Lata Mangeshkar is a (7) _____ . She is from India. She is about 90 years old. She was famous 50 years before now. She is still famous!

What can women do? Anything!

Get Ready to Speak

SPEAKING GOAL:
Ask and Give Personal Information
Personal information is details about you and your life. Ask and give personal information to help someone know more about you.

A Read and listen to the conversation. Underline the W questions. 22

Speaking Tip
Ask for more information using the 5 Ws: *who, what, when, where,* and *why.*

Meeting a New Friend

Dan: Hi. I'm Dan. What's your name?

Allan: Hi! I'm Allan. I'm from Watertown. Where are you from?

Dan: I'm from Watertown, too!

Allan: Really? What school do you go to?

Dan: I go to the Davis School.

Allan: So do I! Who is your teacher?

Dan: Mrs. Smith.

B Look at **A**. What personal information do Dan and Allan ask for? Complete the table.

Who	What	When	Where	Why
teacher				

Speak

C What personal information do you want to know about a friend?
Complete the table. Make notes about the W questions.

Who	What	When	Where	Why

D Now write questions you want to ask. Use your ideas from **C**.
Choose new words, too.

My first question is: _____

_____

My next question is: _____

_____

My next question is: _____

_____

My next question is: _____

_____

My last question is: _____

_____

 With a partner, ask and give personal information.
Use the 5 W questions and take notes.

MY SPEAKING GOAL

☐ I can ask and give personal information.

TOPIC 2

MATH

In My Backpack

MY GOALS

UNIT 3

- Listen to the passage *The First Day of School*
- Listen for facts

UNIT 4

- Listen to the story *Tim's Tablet*
- Listen for opinions

SPEAK

- Agree and disagree

A Look at the picture. What do you see?

1. What are the children doing? What are they using?
2. What do you use in your classroom?

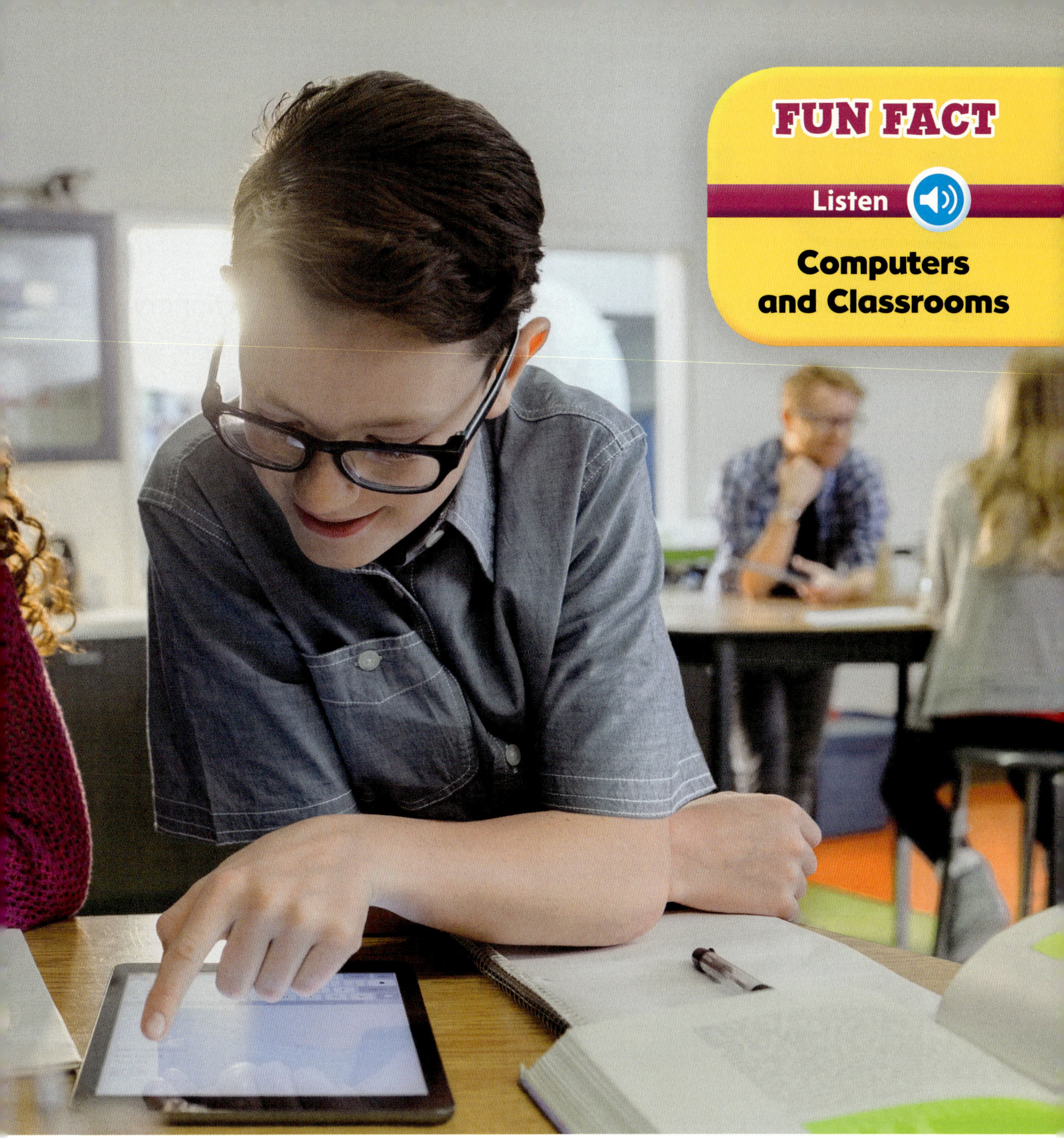

B Listen to the Fun Fact.
Then answer the questions. 🔊 23

1. How many books can a tablet have?

2. Do you like using tablets?
Why or why not?

Think, Pair, Share
In your classroom, what helps you learn?

Get Ready to Listen

Let's learn the **key words**.

A Listen, point, and say. Write the words in your picture dictionary. 24

calculator

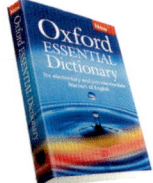
dictionary

folder

scissors

stapler

workbook

B Listen and draw lines. 25

Milo   Anita   Ella   Ben

C Listen and write. 🔊 26

1. _____
2. _____
3. _____
4. _____
5. _____
6. _____

Listen

LISTENING GOAL: Listen for Facts

A fact is something that is true for everyone. For example, *The workbook is blue* is a fact.
Listen for facts to know what is true in a listening.

A Listen. Is the sentence a fact? Complete the sentences with *is*
or *is not.* 🔊 27

1. This _____ a fact.

2. This _____ a fact.

3. This _____ a fact.

The First Day of School

B Listen to the passage *The First Day of School*. What is it about?
Choose the correct picture. 🔊 28

A

B

Now put the sentences in order.

a. The teacher sees that Asha and Abdul are smiling. ☐

b. The teacher says, "Please bring your calculator." ☐

c. The teacher welcomes the students. ☐

What **facts** do
you hear in
the listening?

Think!

• What do you bring to school every day?

Understand

A Think about **The First Day of School**.
What fact did you hear?

Remember!
Facts are true
for everyone.

☐ a. The classroom has scissors.

☐ b. Smiles are great!

B Listen to **The First Day of School** again.
Choose the correct answer. 🔊 29

1. The teacher's name is Mrs. **White** / **Black**.

2. The classroom has a **dictionary** / **calculator** for every student.

3. Students need to bring their folder **every day** / **on Monday**.

4. Every day, students need to bring **three** / **four** things.

5. Asha is **smiling** / **crying**.

C Listen. Complete each sentence with a key word. Then match. 🔊 30

1. Can you please give me the _____

2. I have a _____ in my desk.

3. The _____ is on the desk.

4. My teacher gave me a _____ to use.

a. _____

b. _____

c. _____

d. _____

D Listen to **The First Day of School** again. Who has the things? Work with a partner. Complete the table. 🔊 31

	teacher	classroom	students	Asha and Abdul
1. dictionaries				
2. calculators				
3. workbooks	✔			
4. smiles				

E Look at **D**. Complete the sentences with *has* or *have* and the things.

1.

The teacher ___has workbooks.___

2.
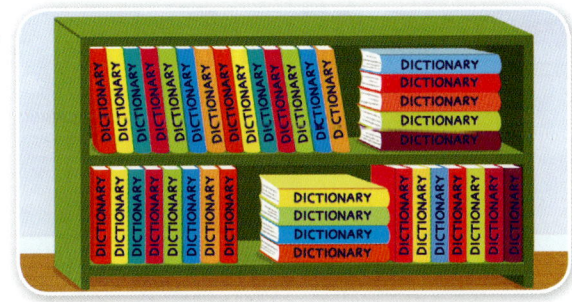
The classroom _____

3.

The students _____
_____

4.

Asha and Abdul _____
_____

MY LISTENING GOALS

☐ I can listen to the passage.

☐ I can listen for facts to know what is true in a listening.

Get Ready to Listen

Let's learn the **key words**.

A Listen, point, and say. Write the words in your picture dictionary. 32

cabinet

drawer

flag

laptop

shelf

tablet

B Listen and number. 33

C Listen and complete the sentences. 34

1. There is a _____ in every classroom.

2. The student is using the _____

3. The scissors are on the _____ or in the _____

4. The boy put his _____ in the _____

Listen

LISTENING GOAL: Listen for Opinions

An opinion is what a person thinks about something. It is not true for everyone. For example, *I think the activities in the workbook are difficult* is an opinion. Listen for opinions to know how people feel.

A Listen. Is the sentence a fact or an opinion? Choose the correct answer. 🔊 35

1. ☐ fact   ☐ opinion
2. ☐ fact   ☐ opinion
3. ☐ fact   ☐ opinion

B Listen to the story *Tim's Tablet*. What is it about? Choose the correct picture. 🔊 36

A ☐

B ☐

Now choose  or ✗.

1. Tim can't find his tablet.   ✔ ✗

2. His classmates help him look for it.   ✔ ✗

3. They find the tablet in a cabinet.   ✔ ✗

> Who says an **opinion**? What is it?

Think!

• How do you feel when you lose something? Why?

Understand

Remember!
Listen for **opinions** to know how people feel.

A Think about **Tim's Tablet**. Are the sentences opinions? Choose **Yes** or **No**.

1. There are ten children.   **Yes**   **No**
2. She thinks he looks sad.   **Yes**   **No**

B Listen to **Tim's Tablet** again. Choose the correct answer. 37

1. Where does Tim look for his tablet?
   ☐ a. in his drawer   ☐ b. in his backpack
2. How many children are there in the class?
   ☐ a. nine   ☐ b. ten
3. Where is Tim's tablet?
   ☐ a. on the teacher's desk ☐ b. at home

C Listen and choose the correct picture. Then write the key word. 38

1.
   ☐ a.   ☐ b.

2.
   ☐ a.   ☐ b.

_____

3.
   ☐ a.   ☐ b.

4.
   ☐ a.   ☐ b.

_____

D Listen to **Tim's Tablet** again. Work with a partner. Complete the diagram. 🔊 39

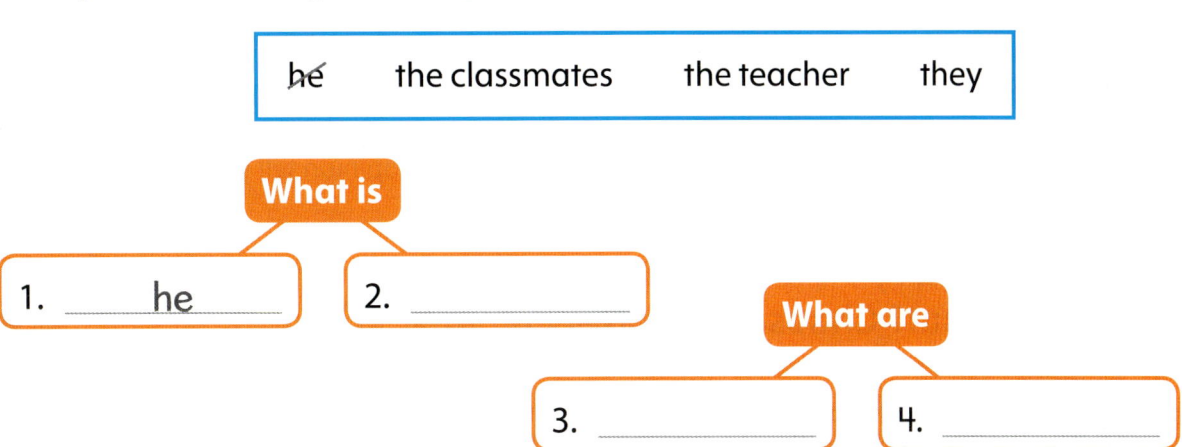

| he | the classmates | the teacher | they |

What is

1. _____he_____   2. _____

What are

3. _____   4. _____

E Look at **D**. Write a question. Use *What* + *is* or *are*.

1.

_____What is_____ he looking for?

2.

_____ the teacher looking for?

3.

_____ they looking for?

4.

_____ the classmates looking for?

MY LISTENING GOALS

☐ I can listen to the story.

☐ I can listen for opinions to know how people feel.

Listening Check

> **Remember!**
> Listen for **facts**. What does a fact tell you? Listen for **opinions**. What does an opinion tell you?

A Listen to the story **Can I Use Your Dictionary?** What is it about? Choose the correct picture. 🔊 40

B Which facts are true? Choose ✔ or ✘.

1. The teacher asks Sal and Cora to be partners. ✔ ✘

2. Sal has his dictionary in class today. ✔ ✘

3. Cora shares her workbook with Sal. ✔ ✘

4. There are no scissors in the cabinet. ✔ ✘

C Which sentences are opinions? Choose ✔ or ✘.

1. Sal asks for Cora's calculator. ✔ ✘

2. Sal thinks Cora is smart. ✔ ✘

3. Sal has everything at home. ✔ ✘

4. Cora thinks Sal is nice. ✔ ✘

Listen to Can I Use Your Dictionary? again.
Choose the correct answer. 🔊 41

1. Who asks Sal and Cora to be partners?

☐ a. Sal   ☐ b. Cora   ☐ c. the teacher

2. Why is Sal happy to be Cora's partner?

☐ a. She's his best friend.   ☐ b. She has a workbook.   ☐ c. She's smart.

3. What does Sal ask Cora for first?

☐ a. her calculator   ☐ b. her workbook   ☐ c. her dictionary

4. What is in the cabinet?

☐ a. workbooks   ☐ b. scissors   ☐ c. dictionaries

5. Where are Sal's things?

☐ a. in class   ☐ b. in his backpack   ☐ c. at home

E **Listen to Can I Use Your Dictionary? again.**
Complete the sentences. 🔊 42

The teacher asks Sal and Cora to be partners.

Sal says, "I'm glad you're my partner, Cora. You're so smart."

Cora says, "Thanks, Sal. You're so nice!"

Sal asks, "Can I use your (1) _____?" Cora says, "Sure!"

Then Sal asks, "Can I see your (2) _____?" Cora says, "OK."

Soon Sal says, "Can I look at your (3) _____?"

Cora says, "OK. But don't ask for my (4) _____ or my

(5) _____. There are some in the (6) _____."

Sal says, "Thanks!"

Cora asks, "Why don't you have anything today?"

Sal says, "Oh. I do have everything." "You do?" asks Cora.

"Yes!" Sal says. "At home!"

Get Ready to Speak

SPEAKING GOAL: Agree and Disagree

You agree with someone when you have the same opinion.
You disagree when you have a different opinion.

A Read and listen to the conversation. Underline the words that show Ana and Ned agree and disagree.  43

> **Speaking Tip**
> Use *you're right* to agree. Use
> *I don't think so* to disagree.

The Important Things

Ana: What are the important things we use in class? What do you think?

Ned: Calculators!

Ana: Really? Why?

Ned: They make math easier!

Ana: I don't think so. I don't think they are important. We can do math without them.

Ned: What do you think is important?

Ana: I think dictionaries are important.

Ned: You're right. Dictionaries are very important.

B Look at **A**. What do Ana and Ned agree and disagree about? Complete the table.

They agree about …	They disagree about …
1.	2.

Speak

C Think about things in your classroom. Are they important or not? Complete the table with your opinion.

Important	Not Important

D Now write about your opinions. Use your ideas from **C**. Choose new words, too. Then draw the important things.

I think _____

_____

_____

I don't think _____

_____

_____

With a partner, talk about things in the classroom. Are they important or not? Ask for your partner's opinions. Do you agree or disagree?

MY SPEAKING GOAL

☐ I can agree and disagree.

TOPIC 3

SOCIAL STUDIES

I Like Your Clothes

MY GOALS

UNIT 5

- Listen to the conversation *Shopping with Mom*
- Listen for preferences

UNIT 6

- Listen to the story *The Little Brother*
- Listen for reasons

SPEAK

- Give preferences

A Look at the picture. What do you see?

1. Where are the girls? What are they doing?

2. Did you last shop for clothes online or in a store? What did you buy?

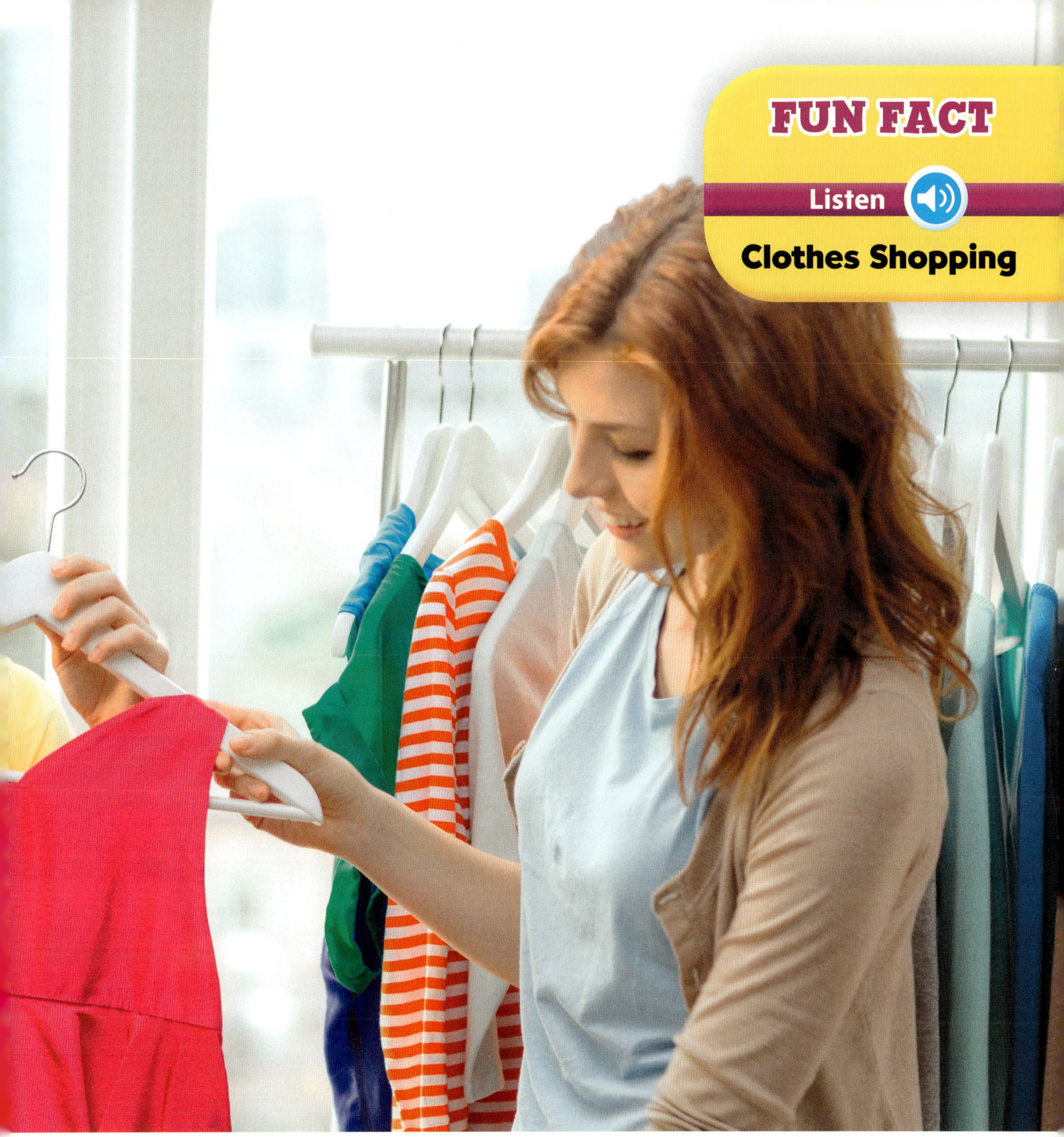

B Listen to the Fun Fact.
Then answer the questions. 🔊 44

1. Why do people like shopping for
   clothes in stores?

2. How do you usually shop?

Think, Pair, Share
Do you like shopping for
clothes? Why or why not?

Get Ready to Listen

Let's learn the **key words**.

A Listen, point, and say. Write the words in your picture dictionary. 45

baseball cap   coat   handbag   shorts   sneakers   swimsuit

B Listen and draw lines. 46

Bess   Lisa   Tom   Jack

C Listen and write. 47

1. _____   2. _____   3. _____

4. _____   5. _____   6. _____

Listen

A preference is when you like one thing more than another thing.
Listen for *I prefer* and *I like* to know about preferences.

A Listen. Choose the correct answer. 🔊 48

1. Jan prefers the **orange handbag** / **pink handbag**.
2. Taro likes the **black coat** / **red coat** more.
3. Asha prefers to wear **shorts** / **pants**.

B Listen to the conversation *Shopping with Mom*.
What is it about? Choose the correct picture. 🔊 49

A

B

Now put the sentences in order.

a. Mali's mom doesn't have enough money. ☐

b. Mali's mom says that the store has so many things. ☐

c. Mali says which shorts she likes. ☐

> What does Mali say she likes? What does her mom prefer?

Think!

• What kind of clothes do you like shopping for?

Understand

A **Think about Shopping with Mom. What does Mali prefer?**

☐ a. the red shorts

☐ b. the blue shorts

> **Remember!**
> You can find **preferences** by listening for the words *I prefer* and *I like*.

B **Listen to Shopping with Mom again.**
Choose the correct answer. 🔊 50

1. Mali's mom says the store has everything from **coats to swimsuits** / **pants to baseball caps**.

2. Mali wants to buy a **baseball cap** / **handbag**.

3. Mali's mom shows Mali red **handbags** / **shorts**.

4. Mali's mom likes the **yellow** / **white** handbag.

5. Mali's mom doesn't have enough **time** / **money**.

C **Listen. Complete each sentence with a key word. Then match.** 🔊 51

1. I wear _____ almost every day.

2. Bring your _____ to the store.

3. Alec and I have the same _____

4. I like your _____

a. _____

b. _____

c. _____

d. _____

D Listen to **Shopping with Mom** again. Do Mali and her mom like the things? Work with a partner. Complete the table. 🔊 52

Do you like the …	Yes	No
1. red shorts		✔
2. blue shorts		
3. white handbag		
4. yellow handbag		

E Look at **D**. Complete the sentences.

1.

Mom: Do you like the red shorts?

Mali: _____No_____ , I _____don't._____

2.

Mom: Do you like the blue shorts?

Mali: _____ , I _____

3.

Mali: Do you like the white handbag?

Mom: _____ , I _____

4.

Mali: Do you like the yellow handbag?

Mom: _____ , I _____

Get Ready to Listen

Let's learn the **key words**.

A Listen, point, and say. Write the words in your picture dictionary. 53

clean

dirty

heavy

light

thick

thin

B Listen and number. 54

C Listen and complete the sentences. 55

1. The backpack is _____

2. The handbag is _____

3. Are the sneakers _____ or _____

4. Your hair is _____ . It isn't _____

Listen

LISTENING GOAL: Listen for Reasons

A reason is why people do something or why something happens.
Listen for *because* to know reasons.

A Listen. Choose ✔ or ✘. 🔊 56

1. ✔ ✘

2. ✔ ✘

3. ✔ ✘

The Little Brother

B Listen to the story *The Little Brother*. What is it about?
Choose the correct picture. 🔊 57

Now choose ✔ or ✘.

1. Gil's shirt is dirty. ✔ ✘

2. The mother changes Gil's shirt. ✔ ✘

3. Gil doesn't like any of his shirts. ✔ ✘

> What are some **reasons** in the passage?

Think!

• What kind of clothes do you like to wear? Why?

Understand

A Think about **The Little Brother**. Do you hear a reason for each of these things? Choose **Yes** or **No**.

1. why Gil needs a new shirt   **Yes**   **No**
2. why Marco likes Gil's shirt   **Yes**   **No**

B Listen to **The Little Brother** again. Choose the correct answer. 🔊 58

1. What is Gil eating?
   ☐ a. chocolate   ☐ b. a banana
2. What color is Gil's shirt?
   ☐ a. blue   ☐ b. purple
3. Why doesn't Gil like the purple shirt?
   ☐ a. It's too thick.   ☐ b. It's too thin.

C Listen and choose the correct picture. Then write the key word. 🔊 59

1.
   ☐ a.   ☐ b.

2.
   ☐ a.   ☐ b.

3.
   ☐ a.   ☐ b.

4.
   ☐ a.   ☐ b.

D Listen to **The Little Brother** again. What is the problem with each shirt? Work with a partner. Complete the diagram. 60

Shirt		Problem
1. blue shirt	→	too dirty
2. _____	→	_____
3. _____	→	_____
4. _____	→	_____

E Look at **D**. Write the problem with each shirt. Use *too*.

1.

The blue shirt is too dirty. _____

_____

2.

_____

_____

3.

_____

_____

4.

_____

_____

MY LISTENING GOALS

☐ I can listen to the story.

☐ I can listen for a reason.

Listening Check

A Listen to the article **What Clothes Do They Wear?**
What is it about? Choose the correct picture. 🔊 61

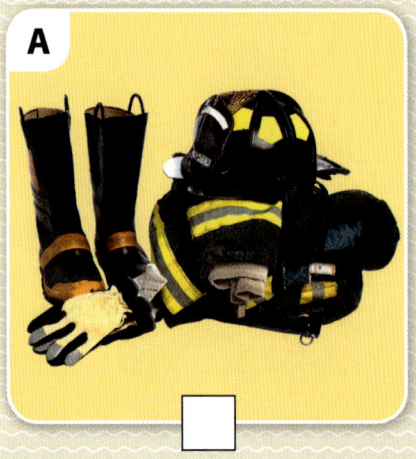
A

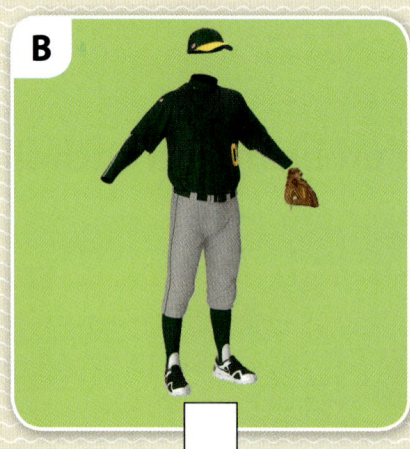
B

C

B What do baseball players prefer? Choose ✔ or ✘.

1. shorts   ✔ ✘
2. long pants   ✔ ✘
3. cleats   ✔ ✘
4. heavy clothes   ✔ ✘

C Why do baseball players wear special clothes? Choose ✔ or ✘.

1. because they are heavy   ✔ ✘
2. because they are light   ✔ ✘
3. because they are easy to run in ✔ ✘
4. because they are warm   ✔ ✘

1. Why do baseball players wear special clothes?
   ☐ a. to get dirty   ☐ b. to play well   ☐ c. to look good

2. What are baseball sneakers called?
   ☐ a. boots   ☐ b. cleats   ☐ c. shoes

3. Why do baseball players wear cleats?
   ☐ a. to look good   ☐ b. to hit the ball   ☐ c. to help them run

4. Baseball clothes are
   ☐ a. light.   ☐ b. heavy.   ☐ c. blue.

5. What don't baseball players wear?
   ☐ a. a shirt   ☐ b. pants   ☐ c. shorts

E Listen to **What Clothes Do They Wear?** again.
Complete the sentences. 🔊 63

Baseball players wear special hats, shoes, and clothes. The players wear these things because they help them play well.

They wear (1) _____ because these hats keep the sun out of their eyes. They wear special kinds of (2) _____ called cleats. They prefer cleats because cleats help them run. They also help them not fall down. Players wear special pants and a shirt. These clothes are not (3) _____. They are very (4) _____. This helps them play and run. Baseball players do not wear (5) _____. Why not? Because their legs get very (6) _____ when they play!

Get Ready to Speak

SPEAKING GOAL: Give Preferences

A preference is liking one thing more than another thing. Give preferences to tell what you like.

A Read and listen to the conversation. Underline the words for giving preferences.  64

> **Speaking Tip**
> Use the words *I prefer* and *I like* with *because* to give preferences.

Ava: I want new sneakers. I want to ask my mom to take me shopping.

Pablo: You can ask her to buy you sneakers online.

Ava: I don't really like shopping on the computer.

Pablo: Why not?

Ava: I prefer to shop in stores.

Pablo: Really? Why?

Ava: Because I like to see things before I buy them. And I like going shopping. Which do you prefer?

Pablo: I'm not sure. I think I like shopping online because it's easy and fast!

Ava: That's true!

B Look at **A**. What do they prefer? Why? Complete the table.

	Shop in store or online?	Why?
1. Pablo	online	
2. Ava		

Speak

C Think about how or where you prefer to shop. Complete the table.

	Shop in store or online?	Why?
You		

D Now write about how or where you like to shop and why. Use your ideas from **C**. Choose new words, too. Then draw something you want to buy.

I want _____

I prefer _____

_____

because _____

_____

I also prefer _____

_____

because _____

_____

 Work with a partner. Tell each other about how or where you like to shop.

MY SPEAKING GOAL

☐ I can give preferences.

TOPIC 4

All Around Town

GEOGRAPHY

MY GOALS

UNIT 7

- Listen to the story *Fun Trip*
- Listen for sequence

UNIT 8

- Listen to the phone message *Come Over!*
- Listen for directions

SPEAK

- Ask for and give directions

 A Look at the picture. What do you see?

1. Where are the people? What are they doing?

2. Name a place you were at with many people. Why were you there?

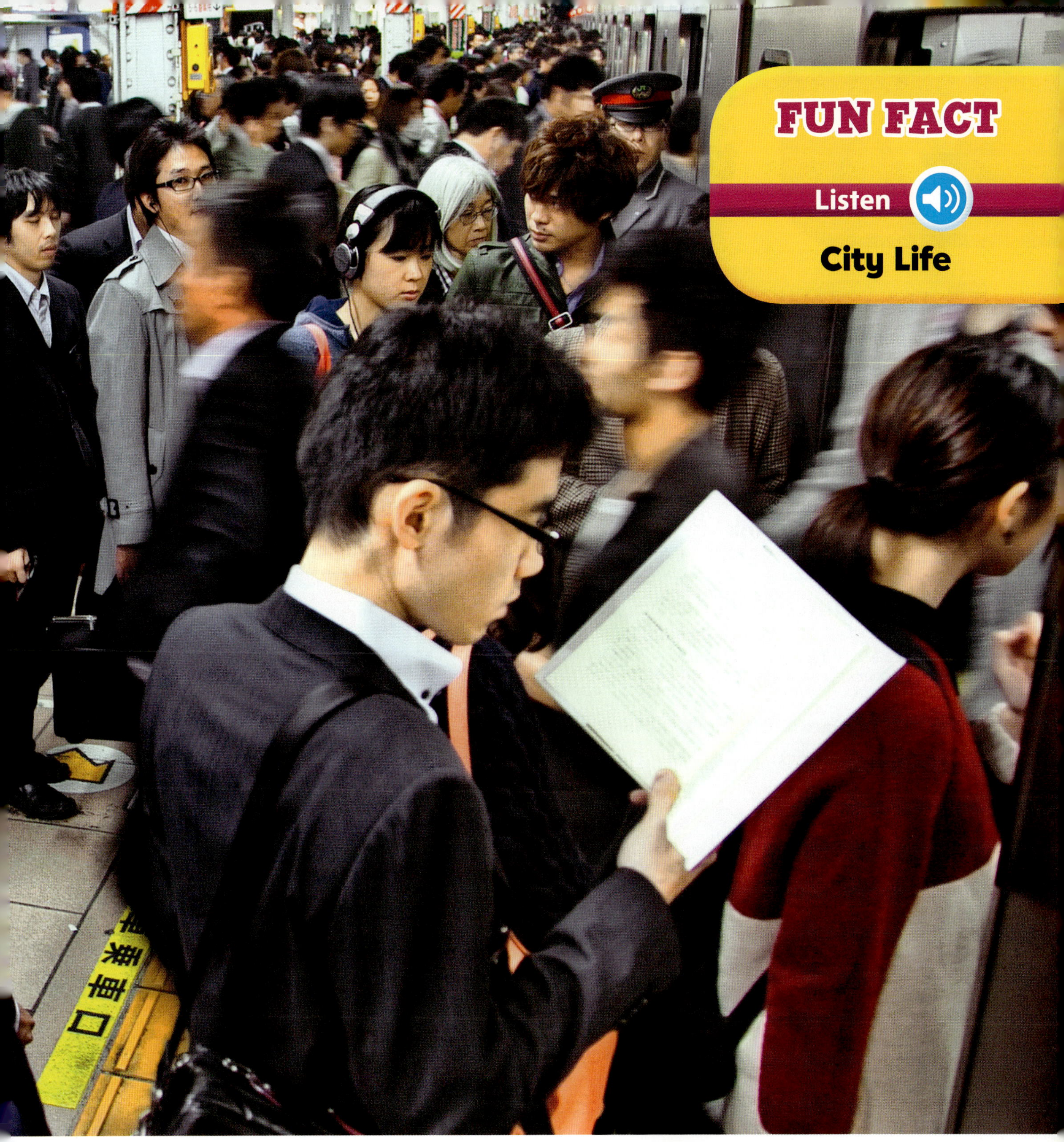

B **Listen to the Fun Fact.**
Then answer the questions. 🔊 65

1. How many people live in Tokyo?

2. What is the special job in Tokyo?
   Is it fun? Why or why not?

Think, Pair, Share
Do you prefer to live in the city or the country? Why?

Get Ready to Listen

Let's learn the **key words**.

A Listen, point, and say. Write the words in your picture dictionary. 66

airport

bank

home

playground

post office

zoo

B Listen and draw lines. 🔊 67

Jen   Prow   Eva   Dan   Ms. Gomez   Mr. Awad

C Listen and write. 🔊 68

1. _____   2. _____   3. _____

4. _____   5. _____   6. _____

Listen

LISTENING GOAL: Listen for Sequence

The sequence is the order things happen. Listen for phrases like *to start*, *before*, and *after* to understand the sequence.

A Listen. Then complete the sentences. 🔊 69

1. To start, Adam's family has _____

2. Before Lin goes to the playground, she goes to _____

3. Jack visited his grandmother after he visited the _____

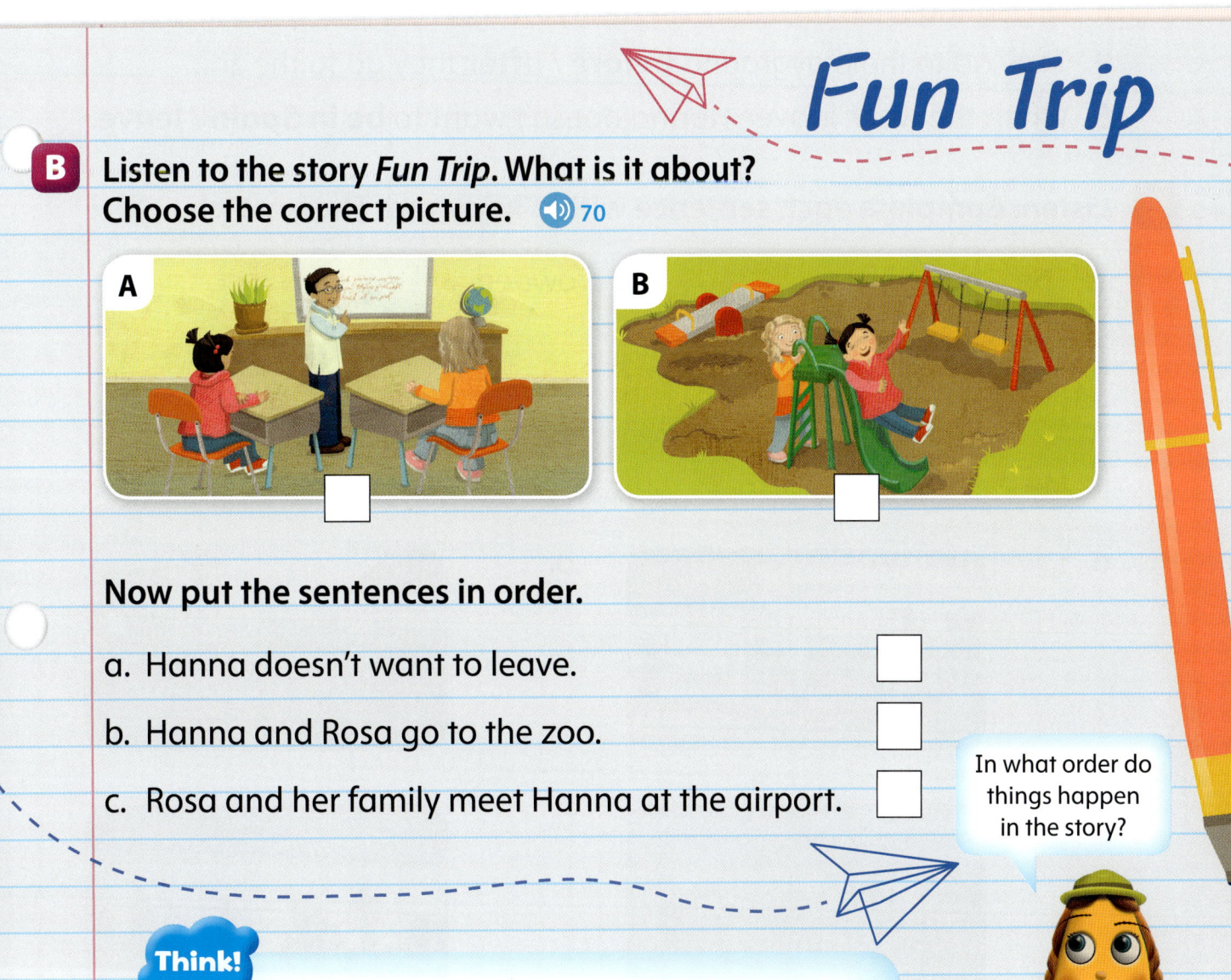

B Listen to the story *Fun Trip*. What is it about?
Choose the correct picture. 🔊 70

Fun Trip

A ☐

B ☐

Now put the sentences in order.

a. Hanna doesn't want to leave. ☐

b. Hanna and Rosa go to the zoo. ☐

c. Rosa and her family meet Hanna at the airport. ☐

In what order do things happen in the story?

Think!

• Do you like to travel to new places? Why or why not?

Understand

A Think about **Fun Trip**. What is the first thing Hanna and Rosa do together?

☐ a. They go to the playground.

☐ b. They go to the post office.

Remember!
Listen for **sequence** words like *to start*, *before*, and *after* to tell you the order things happen.

B Listen to **Fun Trip** again. Choose the correct answer. 🔊 71

1. Hanna and Rosa live in **the same** / **different** countries.

2. At first, Hanna feels **sad** / **happy**.

3. On Hanna's first day, they **do many things** / **do not do many things**.

4. They go to the playground **before** / **after** they go to the zoo.

5. When the week is over, Hanna doesn't want to **be in Spain** / **leave**.

C Listen. Complete each sentence with a key word. Then match. 🔊 72

1. The _____ is crowded.

2. Let's go to the _____ after school.

3. I want to go to the _____ today.

4. My brother is at _____ now.

a. _____

b. _____

c. _____

d. _____

D Listen to **Fun Trip** again. Who goes where? Work with a partner. Complete the table. 🔊 73

	playground	zoo	post office	bank
1. Hanna	✔			
2. Rosa				
3. Rosa's mom				

E Look at **D**. Complete the sentences. Use *go* or *goes* in each sentence.

1.

Hanna and Rosa _____go to_____ _____the playground._____

2.

Hanna and Rosa _____ _____

3.

Rosa's mom _____

4.

Hanna, Rosa, and Rosa's mom _____

MY LISTENING GOALS

☐ I can listen to the story.

☐ I can listen for sequence.

Get Ready to Listen

Let's learn the **key words**.

A Listen, point, and say. Write the words in your picture dictionary. 74

amusement park

apartment

bookstore

museum

restaurant

school

B Listen and number. 🔊 75

C Listen and complete the sentences. 🔊 76

1. The _____ is very large.

2. Where is the _____

3. I want to go to the _____ after _____ today.

4. After we go to the _____ , let's go to a _____

Listen

LISTENING GOAL: Listen for Directions

Directions tell how to go to a place. Listen for direction words and phrases like *go straight*, *walk down*, and *turn left* to know how to go to a place.

A Listen. Choose ✔ or ✘. 🔊 77

1.
   ✔ ✘

2.
   ✔ ✘

3.
   ✔ ✘

Come Over!

B Listen to the phone message *Come Over!*
What is it about? Choose the correct picture. 🔊 78

A ☐   B ☐

Now choose ✔ or ✘.

1. The boy is with the friend he is speaking to.   ✔ ✘

2. He is having a birthday party.   ✔ ✘   What do the **directions** tell you?

3. He is giving directions to his apartment.   ✔ ✘

Think! Think of your last message. Who was the message from? What was it about?

Understand

Remember!
Listen for **direction** words like *right* and *left* to know where to go.

A **Think about Come Over!**
Does Marco give Carla these
directions? Choose **Yes** or **No**.

1. walk down   **Yes**   **No**
2. turn right   **Yes**   **No**

B **Listen to Come Over! again. Choose the correct answer.** 🔊 79

1. What is happening on Friday?
   ☐ a. Marco's test   ☐ b. Marco's birthday party
2. What is next to Marco's apartment?
   ☐ a. a museum   ☐ b. a bookstore
3. Where is everyone going after the amusement park?
   ☐ a. a museum   ☐ b. a restaurant

C **Listen and choose the correct picture. Then write the key word.** 🔊 80

1. ☐ a.   ☐ b.   2. ☐ a.   ☐ b.

3. ☐ a.   ☐ b.   4. ☐ a.   ☐ b.

D Listen to **Come Over!** again. Work with a partner. Complete the table. 🔊 81

Place	Where?	Place
1. museum	across from	restaurant
2. apartment		
3. bookstore		
4. amusement park		

E Look at **D**. Write directions.

1.

The museum is across from a restaurant.

2.

_____

_____

3.

_____

_____

4.

_____

_____

MY LISTENING GOALS

☐ I can listen to the phone message.

☐ I can listen for directions.

Listening Check

A Listen to the story **Things to Do in Town**. What is it about? Choose the correct picture.  82

B Are the things in the correct order? Choose ✔ or ✘.

1. To start, Dana goes to the post office.   ✔ ✘

2. After the post office, she goes to the zoo.   ✔ ✘

3. After the post office, she goes to a restaurant.   ✔ ✘

4. At the end, she goes home.   ✔ ✘

C Are these the right directions for Dana's places? Choose ✔ or ✘.

1. To go to the post office, turn right.   ✔ ✘

2. To go to the post office, go down the street.   ✔ ✘

3. To go to the restaurant, turn left.   ✔ ✘

4. To go to the restaurant, turn right.   ✔ ✘

D Listen to **Things to Do in Town** again.
Choose the correct answer. 🔊 83

1. Where does Dana want to go today?

☐ a. the amusement park
☐ b. the museum
☐ c. the playground

2. Why does Dana need to go to the restaurant?

☐ a. to get a letter
☐ b. to get a box
☐ c. to get some food

3. Where is the post office?

☐ a. next to Dana's house
☐ b. down the street
☐ c. across the street

4. What does Dana hear when she walks into her home?

☐ a. Happy birthday!
☐ b. Surprise!
☐ c. Wow!

5. What is in the box?

☐ a. a toy
☐ b. a balloon
☐ c. a cake

E Listen to **Things to Do in Town** again. Complete the sentences. 🔊 84

Today is Dana's birthday. She wants to go to the

(1) _____ or the (2) _____ . But her mother gives

her things to do in town. "To start, go down the street to the

(3)_____ with this letter. After that, turn right and go to

the (4) _____ next to the (5) _____ to get food."

Dana does these things. Then she goes home. When she goes

into her (6) _____, she hears "Surprise!" It's a party! Her

friends are here! Dana's mother takes the box from her. She

opens it. It's a birthday cake! Dana's mother says, "I wanted

you to be busy. We wanted to get ready for the party!"

Get Ready to Speak

SPEAKING GOAL: Ask for and Give Directions

When you ask for directions, you ask another person how to get to a place. When you give directions, you tell another person how to get to a place.

A Read and listen to the conversation. Underline the action words that tell the man what to do. 🔊 85

Speaking Tip
Use action words like *go*, *turn*, *walk*, and *look* when you give directions.

Man:	Excuse me. Can you give me directions to the post office?
Woman:	Sure. Go down this street. Look for a school.
Man:	OK. Then what?
Woman:	Then turn right on Davis Street.
Man:	Is the post office on Davis Street?
Woman:	No. Go straight down Davis Street to the corner of Davis and Elm streets.
Man:	OK.
Woman:	Turn left onto Elm Street. The post office is on Elm Street between a bookstore and the museum.
Man:	OK. Thank you very much for your help.

B Look at **A**. What directions does the woman give the man? Complete the diagram.

Directions to the Post Office

1. Go down this street. → 2. _____ → 3. _____ → 4. _____

Speak

C Think about a place close to your home. Write directions. Complete the diagram.

Directions to _____

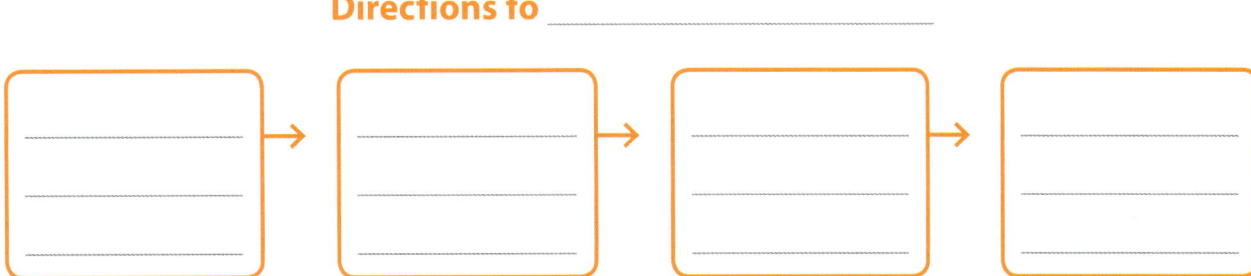

D Now write your directions. Use your ideas from **C**. Choose new words, too. Then draw a map to show the directions to get to this place.

To start, _____

_____

After that, _____

_____

And after that, _____

_____

 Work with a partner. Ask each other about the place you chose. Then ask and give directions.

MY SPEAKING GOAL

☐ I can ask for and give directions.

Busy, Busy, Busy!

MY GOALS

UNIT 9

- Listen to the story *Come to My House*
- Listen for setting

UNIT 10

- Listen to the article *Tips for Busy Kids*
- Listen for descriptions

SPEAK

- Give a description

A Look at the picture. What do you see?

1. Where are the children? What are they doing?
2. Do you think this looks like fun? Why or why not?

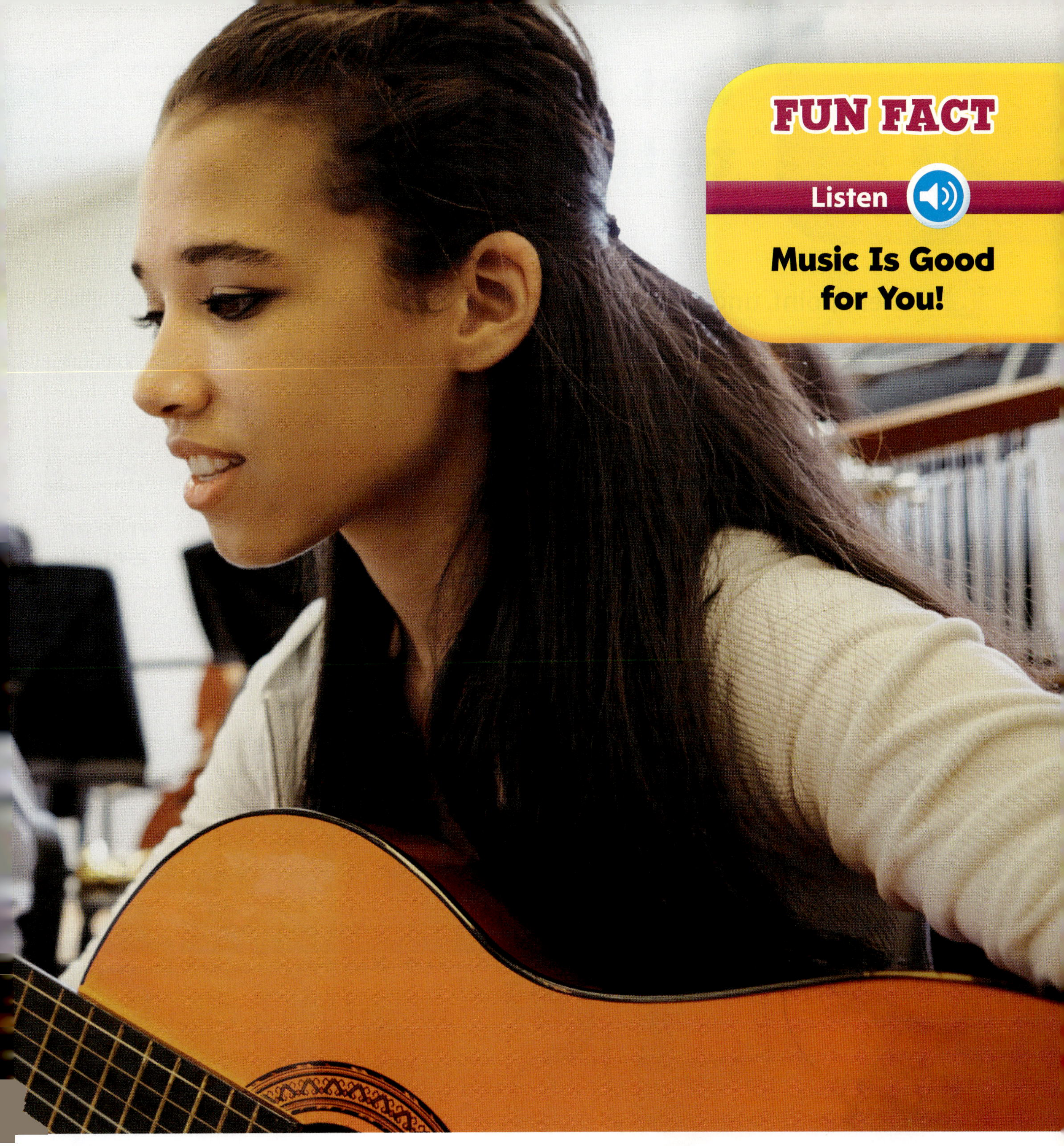

B **Listen to the Fun Fact.**
Then answer the questions. 🔊 86

1. Why is music good for you?

2. What do you like about music?

Think, Pair, Share
What activities do you
do every week?

Get Ready to Listen

Let's learn the **key words**.

A Listen, point, and say. Write the words in your picture dictionary. 🔊 87

| go to swimming class | have a music lesson | practice violin | see a play | take an art class | write an e-mail |

B Listen and draw lines. 🔊 88

Mia   Joe   Dana   Ping

C Listen and write. 🔊 89

1. _____   2. _____   3. _____

4. _____   5. _____   6. _____

Listen

LISTENING GOAL: Listen for Setting

The setting is where and when something happens. Listen for time words like
eight o'clock or *morning* and place words like *house* or *school* to know the setting.

A Listen. What do you know about the setting?
Choose the correct answer. 🔊 90

1. I know about the **time** / **place** / **time and place**.

2. I know about the **time** / **place** / **time and place**.

3. I know about the **time** / **place** / **time and place**.

Come to My House

B Listen to the story *Come to My House*. What is it about?
Choose the correct picture. 🔊 91

Now put the sentences in order.

a. Ray goes to Dan's house at the wrong time. ☐

b. Dan and Ray agree on a time. ☐

c. Ray tells Dan he can't come over on Friday. ☐

> What is the **setting**?
> Does it change?

Think!

• What activities do you do every week?

Get Ready to Listen

Let's learn the **key words**.

A Listen, point, and say. Write the words in your picture dictionary. 95

go for a walk

have fun

listen to music

make a model

play a board game

take a nap

B Listen and number. 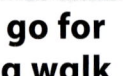 96

C Listen and complete the sentences. 97

1. Ben and his parents _____ every night.

2. I want to _____ of my favorite car.

3. My older sister and her friends like to _____ and _____

4. After they _____, they want to _____

Listen

LISTENING GOAL: Listen for Descriptions

A description tells how something looks, feels, sounds, and tastes.
Listen for description words like *busy*, *fun*, *quiet*, and *good*.

A Listen. Choose ✔ or ✗. 🔊 98

1. ☑✔ ☐✗   2. ☑✔ ☐✗   3. ☑✔ ☐✗

Tips for Busy Kids

B Listen to the article *Tips for Busy Kids*. What is it about?
Choose the correct picture. 🔊 99

A ☐

B ☐

Now choose ✔ or ✗.

1. The article is about how to stay busy.   ☑✔ ☐✗

2. Always being busy makes you feel good.   ☑✔ ☐✗

3. There are different ways to have quiet time.   ☑✔ ☐✗

Think!
• How do you have quiet time?

What **descriptions** are in the article?

Understand

Remember!
To know what something is like, listen for **description words** such as *busy*, *fun*, *quiet*, and *good*.

A Think about **Tips for Busy Kids**.
Are there description words for these things?
Choose **Yes** or **No**.

1. school, friends, and model   **Yes**   **No**
2. flowers, birds, and music   **Yes**   **No**

B Listen to **Tips for Busy Kids** again. Choose the correct answer.  100

1. What can happen when you get very tired?
   ☐ a. You can get bored.   ☐ b. You can get sick.
2. What does the article say you should have every day?
   ☐ a. quiet time   ☐ b. a nap
3. What kind of music does the article talk about?
   ☐ a. loud   ☐ b. beautiful

C Listen and choose the correct picture. Then write the key word. 🔊 101

1.

☐ a.   ☐ b.

2.

☐ a.   ☐ b.

3.

☐ a.   ☐ b.

4.

☐ a.   ☐ b.

D Listen to **Tips for Busy Kids** again. Work with a partner. Complete the table. 🔊 102

Action Word	Description Word	Thing
1. go	nice	walk
2.		board game
3.		music
4.		nap

E Look at **D**. Write sentences using description words.

1.

Go for a nice walk.

2.

 3.

4.

MY LISTENING GOALS

☐ I can listen to the article.

☐ I can listen for descriptions.

Listening Check

A Listen to the radio advertisement **A Place for Fun**. What is it about? Choose the correct picture. 🔊 103

A

B

C

B Which are true statements about the setting? Choose ✔ or ✗.

1. The time is the morning. ✔ ✗
2. The time is the afternoon. ✔ ✗
3. The place is an art class. ✔ ✗
4. The place is a swim class. ✔ ✗

C Which words are used to describe each place? Choose ✔ or ✗.

1. The theater is beautiful. ✔ ✗
2. The pool is small. ✔ ✗
3. The art class is great. ✔ ✗
4. The projects are boring. ✔ ✗

D Listen to **A Place for Fun** again. Choose the correct answer. 🔊 104

1. What is the radio advertisement about?
   ☐ a. a school
   ☐ b. a town center building
   ☐ c. a theater

2. What is something you can do there?
   ☐ a. see a play
   ☐ b. see a movie
   ☐ c. play soccer

3. How many students are in the art class?
   ☐ a. eight
   ☐ b. nine
   ☐ c. ten

4. What does Ryan say about the art projects?
   ☐ a. They are interesting.
   ☐ b. They are difficult.
   ☐ c. They are long.

5. What does Ryan say the students do every week?
   ☐ a. make a model
   ☐ b. have fun
   ☐ c. see a play

E Listen to **A Place for Fun** again. Complete the sentences. 🔊 105

Man: Welcome to our town center building! It's Monday afternoon, and there is so much to do here. You can (1) _____ in our beautiful theater or (2) _____ in our quiet computer room. You can (3) _____ in the music room or (4) _____ in our big, new pool! Let's visit our after-school art class. Ten students are (5) _____ here this afternoon. Let's talk to Ryan. Ryan, can you tell us what you think about this art class?

Ryan: It's great! We do really interesting projects. And every week we (6) _____

Man: Thanks, Ryan! Come down to the town center building and have some fun with us!

Get Ready to Speak

SPEAKING GOAL: Give a Description

A description tells how something looks, feels, sounds, or tastes.
To give a description, use words that give more information.

A Read and listen to the description. Underline the description words.  106

Speaking Tip
Use description words like *hard*, *interesting*, and *small* before a person, place, or thing.

Hi. I'm Greg. I love making interesting models. It takes a lot of time and hard work. But it is fun work.

I started making them when I was five. Those models were small and easy because they only had a few pieces.

I make much more difficult models now. They have many small pieces!

B Look at **A**. What description words does Greg use to describe each of these things? Complete the diagram.

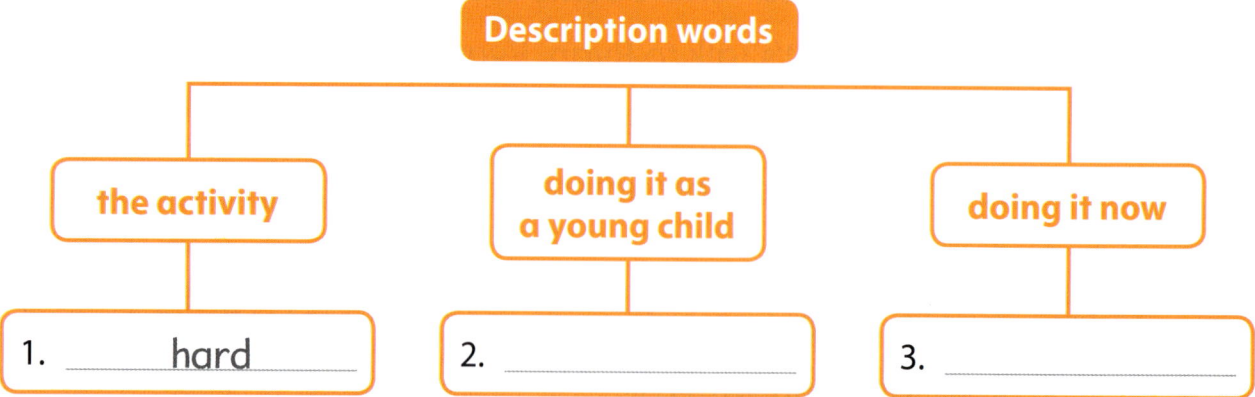

Description words

the activity   doing it as a young child   doing it now

1. ___hard___   2. _____   3. _____

Speak

C Think about your favorite activity. Write description words to describe it. Complete the diagram.

Description words

| your favorite activity | when you started the activity | now |

_____   _____   _____

D Now write a description of your favorite activity. Use your ideas from **C**. Choose new words, too. Then draw the activity.

I love _____

It is _____ and _____

When I started doing this activity, it was

_____

Now it is _____

 Work with a partner. Ask your partner about his or her favorite activity. Then tell your partner about your favorite activity.

MY SPEAKING GOAL

☐ I can give a description.

TOPIC

6

HISTORY

Home Sweet Home

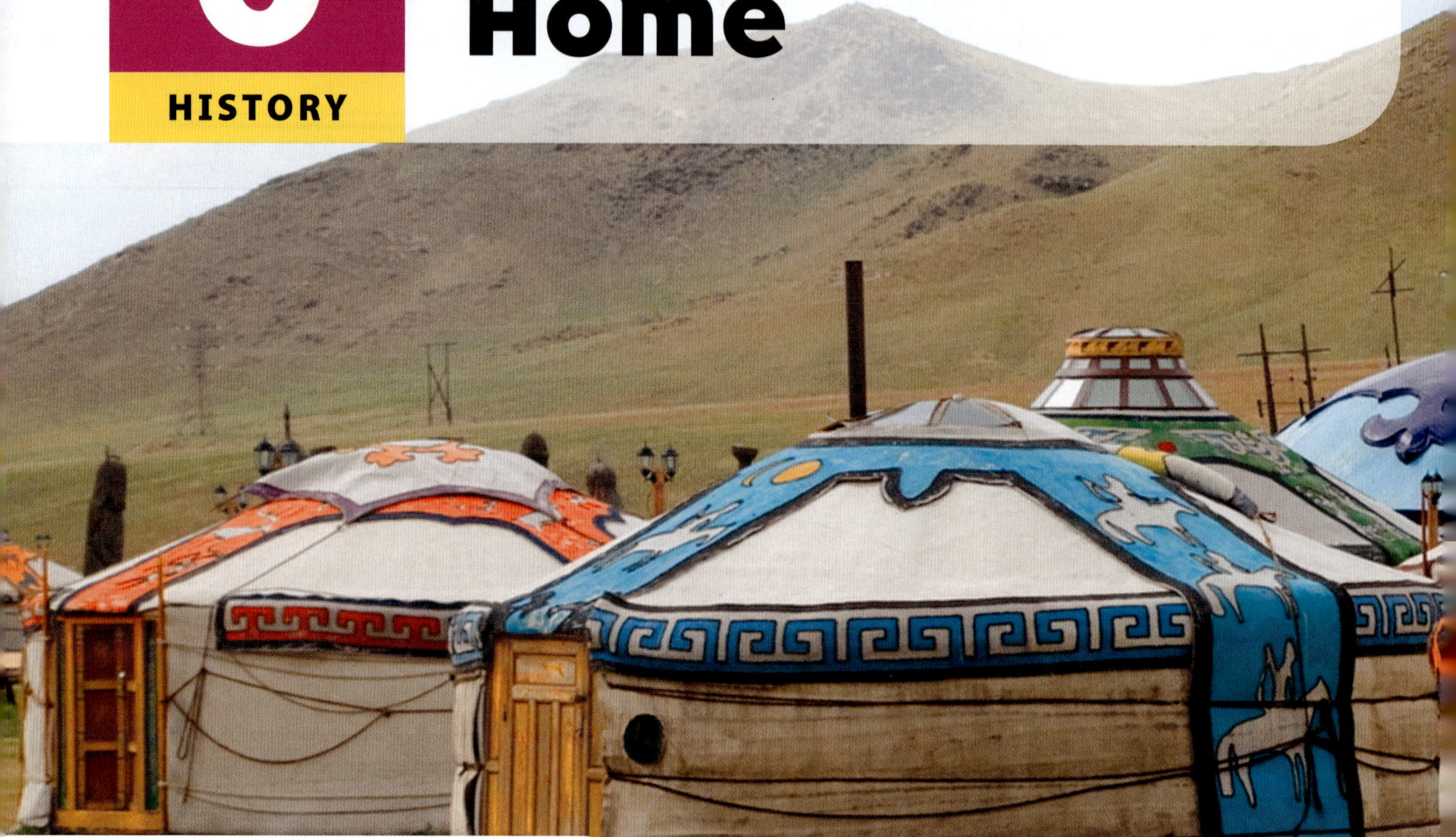

MY GOALS

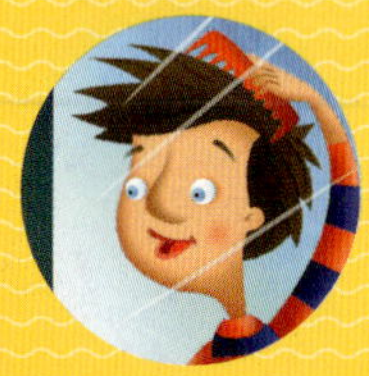

UNIT 11

- Listen to the story *The Mirror*
- Listen for what is similar

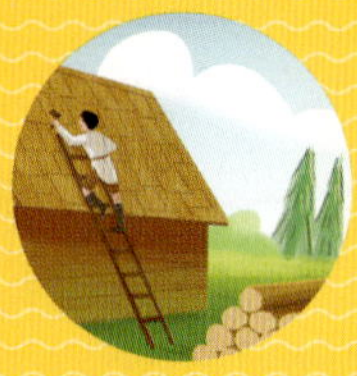

UNIT 12

- Listen to the article *Then and Now*
- Listen for what is different

SPEAK

- Make a comparison

A **Look at the picture. What do you see?**

1. Where is this?
2. Do you want to live there? Why or why not?

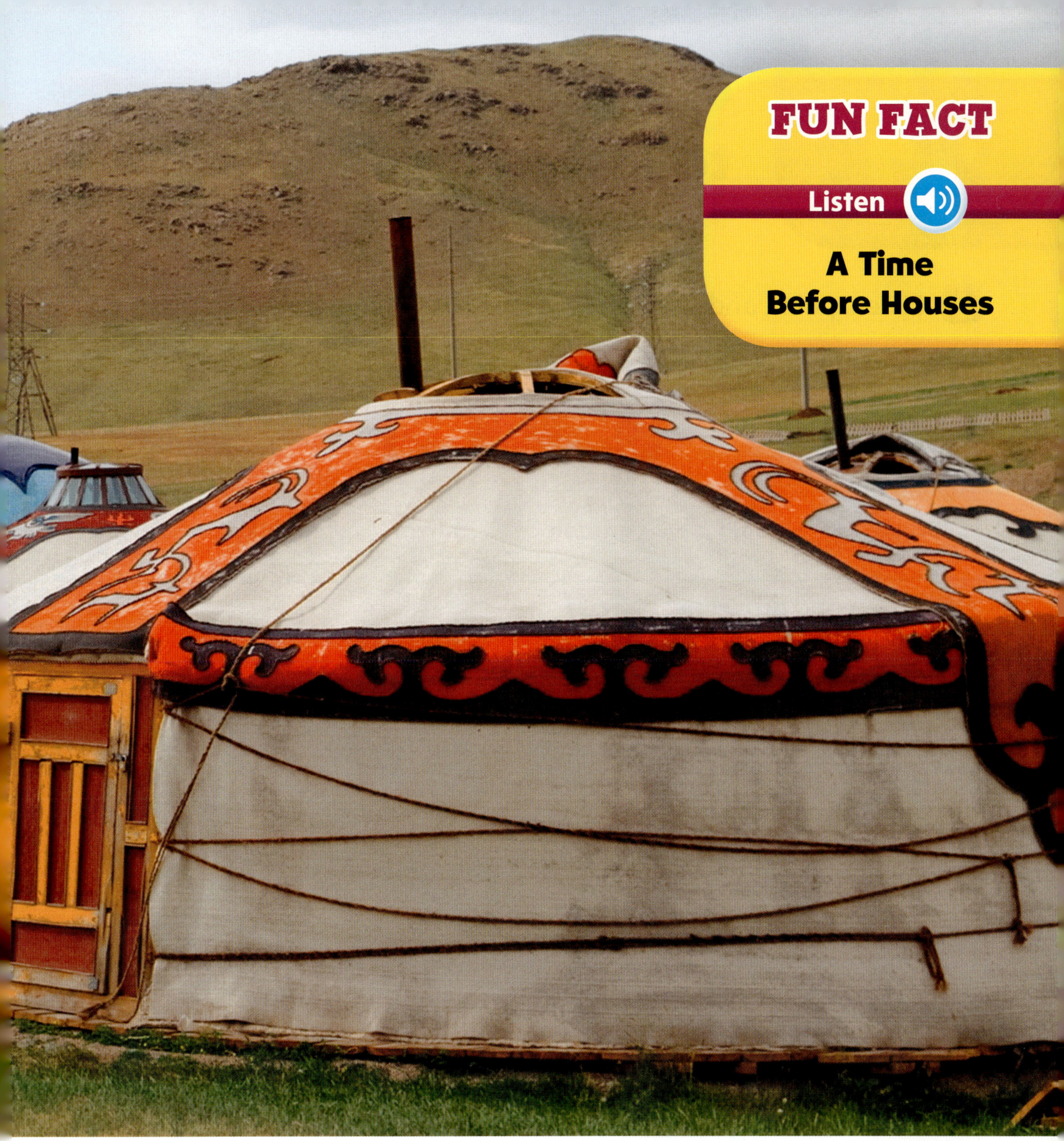

Listen

A Time Before Houses

B Listen to the Fun Fact. Then answer the questions. 🔊 107

1. How did people live thousands of years before now?

2. Do you think this was a good way to live? Why or why not?

Think, Pair, Share
What is your home like?

Get Ready to Listen

Let's learn the **key words**.

A Listen, point, and say. Write the words in your picture dictionary.  108

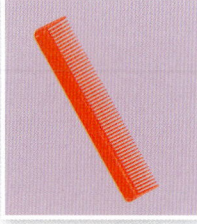

| brush | comb | garden | mirror | sink | stairs |

B Listen and draw lines.  109

Sara   Joy   Mark   Leo

C Listen and write.  110

1. _____
2. _____
3. _____
4. _____
5. _____
6. _____

Listen

LISTENING GOAL: Listen for What Is Similar

When two things are almost the same, they are similar.
Listen for words like *both*, *too*, and *also* to find what is similar.

A **Listen. Then complete the sentences.** 🔊 111

1. Sofia and Daniel both live in _____ houses.

2. Aisha and Jess both have _____ people in their family.

3. We both grow _____ in our garden.

The Mirror

B **Listen to the story *The Mirror*. What is it about? Choose the correct picture.** 🔊 112

A

B

Now put the sentences in order.

What things are similar in the story?

a. Peter moves to a new home.

b. Peter sees that he is the boy in the mirror.

c. Peter sees another boy and runs away.

Think!

• What do you think is funny about the story?

Understand

A Think about **The Mirror**.
How are Peter and the other boy similar?

☐ a. They both have blue eyes, a big nose, and brown hair.

☐ b. They both have blue eyes, small ears, and blond hair.

B Listen to **The Mirror** again. Choose the correct answer.  113

1. Peter sees **a man** / **another boy** in the mirror.

2. The boy has **big** / **small** ears.

3. The boy has **blond** / **brown** hair.

4. Peter **talks to** / **runs away from** the boy.

5. Peter sees that he is looking in the **sink** / **mirror**.

C Listen. Complete each sentence with a key word. Then match.  114

1. I like your _____

2. Where is the _____

3. I have a black _____, too.

4. That is a small _____

a. _____

b. _____

c. _____

d. _____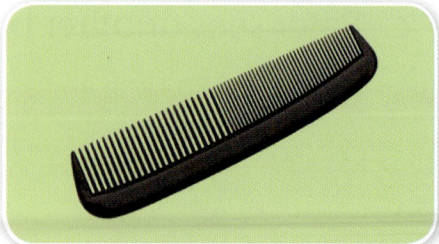

D Listen to **The Mirror** again. Work with a partner. Complete the diagram. 🔊 115

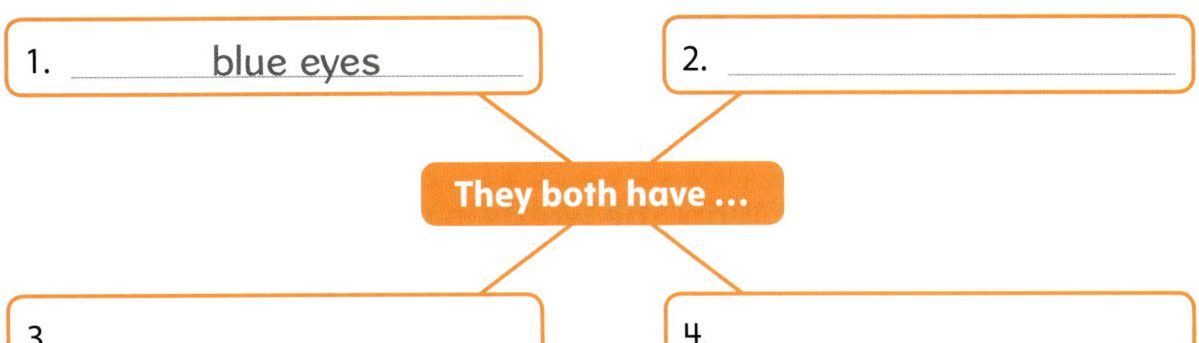

1. _____ blue eyes _____

2. _____

They both have …

3. _____

4. _____

E Look at **D**. Complete the sentences. Use *Peter and the boy both have.*

1.

Peter and the boy both
have blue eyes.

2.

_____

_____

3.

_____

_____

4.

_____

_____

MY LISTENING GOALS

☐ I can listen to the story.

☐ I can listen for what is similar.

Get Ready to Listen

Let's learn the **key words**.

A Listen, point, and say. Write the words in your picture dictionary.  116

armchair

bathtub

oven

refrigerator

rug

sofa

B Listen and number. 117

C Listen and complete the sentences. 118

1. Ed doesn't have a _____ in his house.

2. That _____ is very nice.

3. We use our _____ and _____ every day.

4. We have the same _____ and _____

Listen

When two things are not the same, they are different. Listen for words like *but*, *not*, and *unlike* to find what is different.

A Listen. Choose ✔ or ✘. 🔊 119

1.  ✔ ✘

2.  ✔ ✘

3.  ✔ ✘

Then and Now

B Listen to the article *Then and Now*. What is it about?
Choose the correct picture. 🔊 120

A

B

Now choose ✔ or ✘.

1. The article talks about homes now and homes in 1500. ✔ ✘

2. The article says many things are the same now and in 1500. ✔ ✘

3. People cooked food different ways in 1500. ✔ ✘

Think!
Do you want to live in 1500?
Why or why not?

How are the things in our homes **different** from 1500?

Understand

Remember!
Listen for words like *but*, *not*, and *unlike* to find what is **different**.

A Think about **Then and Now**. Did people do these things in 1500? Choose **Yes** or **No**.

1. People kept food cold with no refrigerators. **Yes   No**
2. People cooked food in ovens. **Yes   No**

B Listen to **Then and Now** again. Choose the correct answer. 121

1. What does the article say looks nice in our homes?
   ☐ a. sofas   ☐ b. rugs

2. In 1500, what did people sit on?
   ☐ a. wood chairs   ☐ b. sofas

3. What did people wash with in 1500?
   ☐ a. rain and a leaf   ☐ b. water and an old piece of clothing

C Listen and choose the correct picture. Then write the key word. 122

1.
   ☐ a.   ☐ b.

2.
   ☐ a.   ☐ b.

3.
   ☐ a.   ☐ b.

4.
   ☐ a.   ☐ b.

D Listen to **Then and Now** again. Work with a partner.
Complete the table. 🔊 123

Today	In 1500
ovens	1. fire
refrigerators	2.
sofas	3.
bathtubs	4.

E Look at **D**. Write. Use *but*.

1.

Today people use ovens,

but in 1500 they used fire.

2.

Today people use refrigerators,

_____

3.

Today people use sofas,

_____

4.

Today people use bathtubs,

_____

MY LISTENING GOALS

☐ I can listen to the article.

☐ I can listen for what is different.

Listening Check

Remember!
Listen for words like *both*, *too*, and *also* to know what is **similar**. Listen for words like *but*, *not*, and *unlike* to know what is **different**.

A Listen to the passage **Just Like Us**. What is it about? Choose the correct picture. 🔊 124

A	B	C
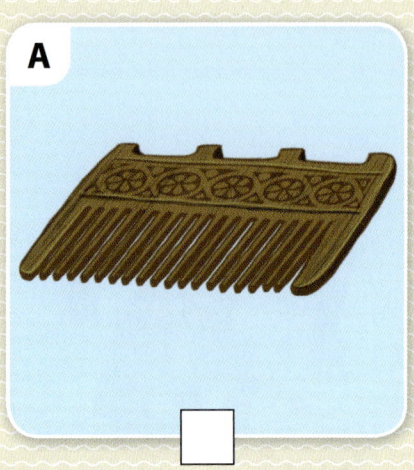		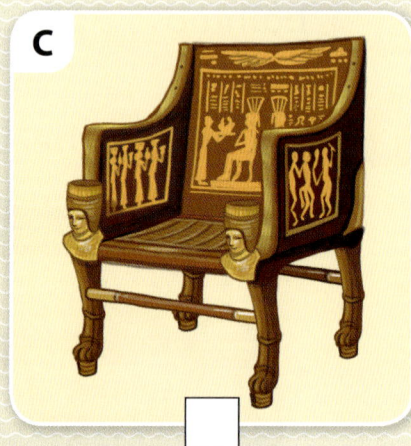
☐	☐	☐

B How were people in Egypt 5,000 years before now similar to us? Choose ✔ or ✘.

1. They had refrigerators. ✔ ✘
2. They wanted to look good. ✔ ✘
3. They had bathtubs. ✔ ✘
4. They had gardens. ✔ ✘

C How were people in Egypt different from us? Choose ✔ or ✘.

1. They cooked with different ovens. ✔ ✘
2. They used combs. ✔ ✘
3. They washed in rivers. ✔ ✘
4. They used mirrors. ✔ ✘

D Listen to Just Like Us again. Choose the correct answer. 🔊 125

1. People in Egypt 5,000 years before now were
   - ☐ a. very different from us.
   - ☐ b. a little different from us.
   - ☐ c. not different from us.

2. What does the passage say people in Egypt 5,000 years before now cared about?
   - ☐ a. how they looked
   - ☐ b. how they cooked
   - ☐ c. how they walked

3. For combs, people in Egypt 5,000 years before now used
   - ☐ a. parts of trees.
   - ☐ b. food.
   - ☐ c. their hands.

4. What is the same about us and people in Egypt 5,000 years before now?
   - ☐ a. using ovens
   - ☐ b. using bathtubs
   - ☐ c. using combs

5. To wash their bodies, people in Egypt 5,000 years before now used
   - ☐ a. rivers.
   - ☐ b. bathtubs.
   - ☐ c. sinks.

E Listen to Just Like Us again. Complete the sentences. 🔊 126

People in Egypt 5,000 years before now were different from us in many ways. Their

(1) _____ were very different. They didn't have

(2) _____. But they were similar to us too.

We want to look good. This was true for them too!

We use (3) _____. They used them too.

They used parts of trees for their combs. There were

no (4) _____, but they washed themselves in

the river. They also used (5) _____. We have

(6) _____, and they did too.

In many ways, they were just like us!

Get Ready to Speak

SPEAKING GOAL: Make a Comparison

When you make a comparison, you say how one thing is like or not like another.

A Read and listen to the passage. Underline the phrases for making comparisons. 🔊 127

> **Speaking Tip**
> To make a comparison, use phrases like *as well*, *similarly*, and *on the other hand*.

Welcome Home   by Hoshi Ito

My home is new. My family just moved to it last year. In some ways, it is like our old home. There was a garden at the back of our old home. Similarly, there is a garden at the back of my new home. On the other hand, some things are different in the new home. In the old home, there was a very big living room with big windows. The living room in our new home is small. On the other hand, I have my own room for the first time in the new home. I'm very excited about that!

B Look at **A**. How does Hoshi compare her new home to her old home? Complete the diagram.

Hoshi's New Home
1. small living room
2. _____

Both
3. _____

Hoshi's Old Home
4. _____
5. _____

Speak

C Think about your home. Compare it to an old home or a friend's home. Complete the diagram.

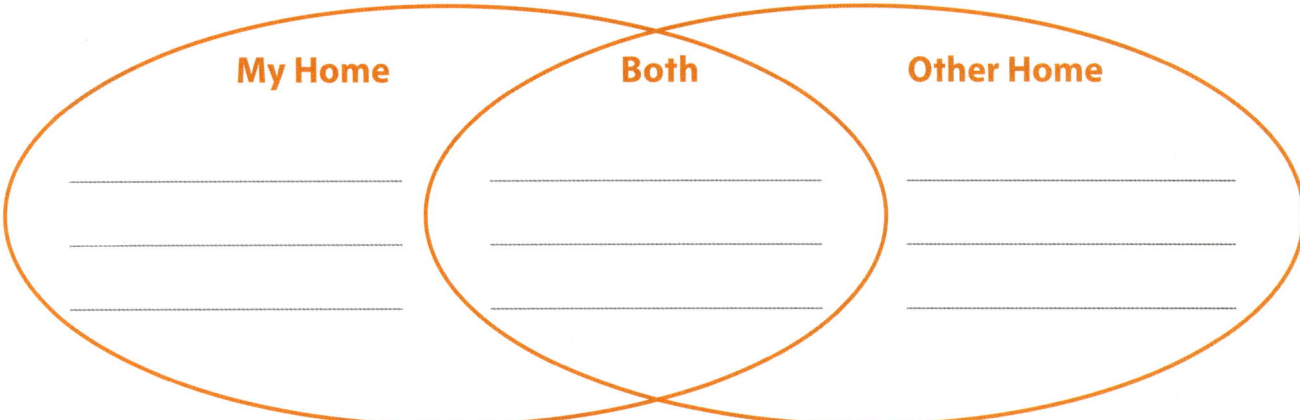

My Home   **Both**   **Other Home**

D Now write about your home. Use your ideas from **C**. Choose new words, too. Then draw your home.

My home is _____

_____

Similarly, _____

_____

On the other hand, _____

_____

 Ask your partner about his or her home. Then tell about your home and compare it to another home you know.

MY SPEAKING GOAL

☐ I can make a comparison.

Oxford Skills World

Listening 3

with Speaking

Workbook

Jill Korey O'Sullivan

OXFORD
UNIVERSITY PRESS

Listen

LISTENING GOAL:
Listen and Take Notes

Remember!
Notes are words or phrases you write down as you listen. **Notes** help you remember important information.

A Listen to the story **The Zookeeper's Problem.** What is it about? Take notes. 🔊 128

Notes

_____

_____

_____

_____

B Think about **The Zookeeper's Problem.** What is a good note? Choose ✔ or ✗.

1. The panda won't come out. ✔ ✗

2. One of the visitors is a news reporter. ✔ ✗

3. The musician is a woman. ✔ ✗

C Listen to **The Zookeeper's Problem** again. Choose the correct answer. 🔊 129

1. Where is the panda?
   ✔ a. in a van　　☐ b. in a car　　☐ c. in a box

2. What does the zookeeper bring the animal?
   ☐ a. a toy　　☐ b. a friend　　☐ c. food

3. Who helps?
   ☐ a. the news reporter　☐ b. a visitor　　☐ c. another animal

4. What does the musician play?
   ☐ a. a fun game　　☐ b. beautiful music　☐ c. loud music

D Listen and write the word. Then choose the correct picture. 🔊 130

1. _____tailor_____   2. _____

☑ a.   ☐ b.   ☐ a.   ☐ b.

3. _____   4. _____

☐ a.   ☐ b.   ☐ a.   ☐ b.

E Complete the sentences.

| news reporter | ~~driver~~ | musician | judge | tailor | scientist |

1. The _____driver_____ knows all of the roads in the neighborhood.

2. The _____ plays the drums and the piano.

3. The _____ studies animals.

4. The _____ can fix your pants.

F Unscramble and write.

1. g e d j u

_____judge_____

2. e i r v d r

_____

3. c s t i e n t i s

_____

4. o r i l t a

_____

Listen

LISTENING GOAL:
Listen for the 5 Ws

Remember!
Asking yourself the **5 Ws** after you listen will help you know the most important information.

A Listen to the passage **Mechanic to Astronaut**. Then put the pictures in order. 🔊 131

A

1

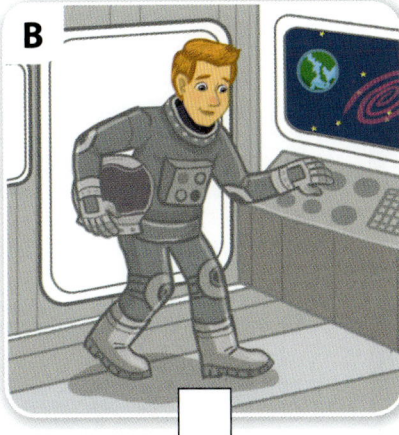

B

C

B Think about **Mechanic to Astronaut**. Which W questions are answered in the story? Choose ✔ or ✘.

1. What do mechanics do?   ✔   ✘

2. Where did he take the test?   ✔   ✘

3. When is he in space?   ✔   ✘

C Listen to **Mechanic to Astronaut** again. Choose Yes or No. 🔊 132

1. Andrew Jay Feustel fixed buses.   **Yes**   **No**

2. He wanted to be an astronaut.   **Yes**   **No**

3. Now he is a news reporter.   **Yes**   **No**

4. He lives in space.   **Yes**   **No**

5. He works with scientists.   **Yes**   **No**

6. He fixes things in space.   **Yes**   **No**

D Listen. Then read and choose the correct answer. 🔊 133

1. Who writes many books?

a. 　　b. 　　c.

2. Who has a dollar?

a. 　　b. 　　c.

3. Who works in a factory?

a. 　　b. 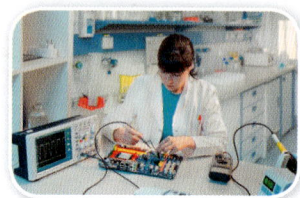　　c.

E Complete the missing words.

1. Many people are listening to the _singer._

2. The _a_____ is in space.

3. The _m_____ is fixing the car.

4. The _e_____ is helping to build a bridge.

> **Remember!**
> Ask for more information using the
> **5 Ws**: who, what, when, where, and why.

Speak

Circle the W words in the questions. Then think of your
own questions with W words. Tell your partner.

Who is she?

What is her job?

Where does she work?

Listen

LISTENING GOAL:
Listen for Facts

A Listen to the passage **Before Calculators**.
What do you hear about? Choose ✔ or ✘. 🔊 134

1.

the stapler   ☑ ✔   ☐ ✘

2.

the abacus   ☑ ✔   ☐ ✘

B Think about **Before Calculators**. What facts do you hear?
Choose ✔ or ✘.

1. We use a dictionary to learn new words.   ☑ ✔   ☐ ✘

2. There were calculators before abacuses.   ☑ ✔   ☐ ✘

3. An abacus has sticks.   ☑ ✔   ☐ ✘

C Listen to **Before Calculators** again. Choose the correct answer. 🔊 135

1. What do we use to do math today?
   ☐ a. an abacus   ☐ b. a calculator   ☐ c. a dictionary

2. Where was the abacus used?
   ☐ a. Thailand   ☐ b. Italy   ☐ c. Egypt

3. What is an abacus made of?
   ☐ a. sticks and beads   ☐ b. stones and beads   ☐ c. beads only

4. How many beads are on each stick?
   ☐ a. five   ☐ b. seven   ☐ c. one

D Listen and write the word. Then choose the correct picture. 🔊 136

1. _____

☐ a.   ☐ b.

2. _____

☐ a.   ☐ b.

3. _____

☐ a.   ☐ b.

4. _____

☐ a.   ☐ b.

E Complete the sentences.

| workbook | folder | dictionary | calculator | stapler | scissors |

1. The students write their homework in their _____

2. I use a _____ to help me with math.

3. You can use _____ to cut the paper.

4. I put all my work in my _____

F Unscramble and write.

1. i o c t d i r y n a

_____

2. a t p r l s e

_____

3. o f r e l d

_____

4. k o b o r w o k

_____

Listen

LISTENING GOAL:
Listen for Opinions

Remember!
An **opinion** is what a person thinks about something. It is not true for everyone. Listen for **opinions** to know how people feel.

A Listen to the story **The Visit**. Then put the pictures in order. 🔊 137

A

B

SEARCH
China

C

B Think about **The Visit**. Which is an opinion? Choose ✔ or ✘.

1. They open a laptop.   ✔   ✘

2. China was very interesting.   ✔   ✘

3. They fall asleep again.   ✔   ✘

C Listen to **The Visit** again. Choose Yes or No. 🔊 138

1. Jen and Al are studying China.   **Yes   No**

2. They are using a tablet.   **Yes   No**

3. They wake up in China.   **Yes   No**

4. The students ask questions about Brazil.   **Yes   No**

5. Al and Jen think China was boring.   **Yes   No**

6. They put the laptop away.   **Yes   No**

D Listen. Then read and choose the correct answer. 🔊 139

1. What does each child in class have?

a.  b.  c.

2. What is on the wall of the classroom?

a.  b.  c.

3. Where are the books?

a.  b.  c.

E Complete the missing words.

1. My country's f_____ is red and white.

2. He uses the Internet on his l_____

3. What is in the d_____

4. The workbooks are in the c_____

Speak

Remember!
Use phrases like *you're right* to **agree** and *I don't think so* to **disagree**.

Circle the phrase that shows a person agrees.
Underline the phrase that shows a person disagrees.
Then tell a partner your opinion.

Beth: I like using laptops in class. I think they help us learn.

John: You're right. They are helpful!

Sara: I don't think so. I think tablets are more helpful.

Listen

LISTENING GOAL:
Listen for Preferences

Remember!
Listen for *I prefer* and *I like* to know about **preferences**.

A Listen to the article **Clothing Then and Now**. What do you hear about? Choose ✔ or ✗. 🔊 140

1.

clothes in 1980   ✔ ✗

2.

clothes in 1890   ✔ ✗

B Think about **Clothing Then and Now**. What clothes did people prefer in 1890? Choose ✔ or ✗.

1. They liked long coats.   ✔ ✗

2. They liked blue coats.   ✔ ✗

3. They liked sneakers.   ✔ ✗

C Listen to **Clothing Then and Now** again. Choose the correct answer. 🔊 141

1. In 1890, people liked _____ hats.
   ☐ a. small   ☐ b. warm   ☐ c. big

2. Today, people wear _____
   ☐ a. heavy hats.   ☐ b. small hats.   ☐ c. big hats.

3. There were no _____ in 1890.
   ☐ a. handbags   ☐ b. sneakers   ☐ c. bathing suits

4. In 1890, most coats were _____
   ☐ a. black.   ☐ b. blue.   ☐ c. short.

D Listen and write the word. Then choose the correct picture. 🔊 142

1. _____

☐ a.　　　☐ b.

2. _____

☐ a.　　　☐ b.

3. _____

☐ a.　　　☐ b.

4. _____

☐ a.　　　☐ b.

E Complete the sentences.

| handbag　coat　baseball cap　sneakers　swimsuit　shorts |

1. I can run fast with these _____

2. I can't go in the water because I don't have a _____

3. My mother has her keys and her money in her _____

4. It is too hot to wear a _____

F Unscramble and write.

1. u w i m s i t s

_____

2. o t s h r s

_____

3. e a l b l a s b a p c

_____

4. a d g b a n h

_____

Listen

LISTENING GOAL:
Listen for Reasons

A Listen to the story **The New Coat**. Then put the pictures in order. 143

A

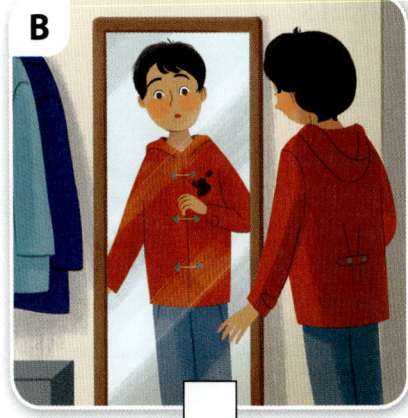

B

C

B Think about **The New Coat**. What are some of the reasons you hear? Choose ✔ or ✘.

1. Amal thinks the coat is heavy because he's wearing two coats.

2. Amal thinks the coat is dirty because the mirror is dirty.

3. Amal's father laughs because the coat is big.

C Listen to **The New Coat** again. Choose Yes or No. 144

1. Amal goes shopping for new sneakers. **Yes** **No**

2. Amal goes shopping with his father. **Yes** **No**

3. Amal's father asks him to try on a coat. **Yes** **No**

4. Amal tries on the coat over his own coat. **Yes** **No**

5. The coat is dirty. **Yes** **No**

6. The mirror is dirty. **Yes** **No**

D **Listen. Then read and choose the correct answer.** 🔊 145

1. What is Jan's new book like?

   a.    b.    c.

2. How are Taro's sneakers?

   a.    b.    c.

3. What are my pants like?

   a.    b.    c.

E **Write the missing letters.**

1. I'm cold because my coat is too t_____

2. My mother just washed these shorts, so they're c_____

3. You can't wear d_____ clothes to school.

4. This workbook has a lot of pages. It's very t_____

Speak

Remember!
Use the words *I prefer* and *I like*
with *because* to give **preferences**.

Circle the words *prefer*, *like*, and *because* in
the sentences. Then think of your own sentence
to give preferences. Tell your partner.

I like the blue shorts because they are my favorite color.

My mother prefers to shop online because it is fast.

Listen

LISTENING GOAL:
Listen for Sequence

Remember!
The **sequence** is the order things happen. Listen for **sequence** words to understand order.

A Listen to the story **Where Is It?** What do you hear about? Choose ✔ or ✘. 🔊 146

1.

Rabbit and her books   ✔ ✘

2.

Rabbit and her gold   ✔ ✘

B Think about **Where Is It?** What is the sequence of the story? Choose ✔ or ✘.

1. To start, Wolf looks for the gold at the zoo.   ✔ ✘

2. To start, Wolf looks for the gold in Rabbit's home.   ✔ ✘

3. After that, Wolf looks for the gold at the zoo.   ✔ ✘

C Listen to **Where Is It?** again. Choose the correct answer. 🔊 147

1. At the start of the story, where does Rabbit say her gold is?
   ☐ a. in the bank   ☐ b. in a safe place   ☐ c. at the zoo

2. After looking for the gold in Rabbit's home, where does Wolf look next?
   ☐ a. at the zoo   ☐ b. at the playground   ☐ c. in the bank

3. Who does Wolf see at the zoo?
   ☐ a. Lion   ☐ b. Bear   ☐ c. Zebra

4. Where does Rabbit keep her gold?
   ☐ a. at her home   ☐ b. at the zoo   ☐ c. at the bank

D Listen and write the word. Then choose the correct picture. 🔊 148

1. _____

☐ a.   ☐ b.

2. _____

☐ a.   ☐ b.

3. _____

☐ a.   ☐ b.

4. _____

☐ a.   ☐ b.

E Complete the sentences.

| airport   zoo   home   post office   bank   playground |

1. People put money in the _____

2. You can fly to many places from the _____

3. I like to watch TV and be with my family at _____

4. There are many animals at the _____

F Unscramble and write.

1. o u g r n d a y p l

_____

2. s p o t c e f i o f

_____

3. p o r t i r a

_____

4. n a b k

_____

Listen

LISTENING GOAL:
Listen for Directions

A Listen to the article **The National Museum of Korea**.
Then put the pictures in order. 🔊 149

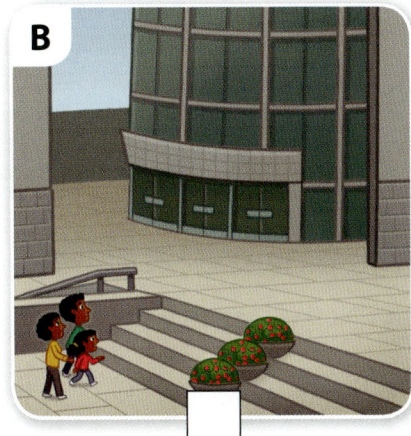

B Think about **The National Museum of Korea**. What are some of the directions you hear? Choose ✔ or ✘.

1. To go to the children's museum, go across the street. ✔ ✘

2. To go to the children's museum, walk straight down the long hall. ✔ ✘

3. To go to the restaurant, go downstairs. ✔ ✘

C Listen to **The National Museum of Korea** again.
Choose **Yes** or **No**. 🔊 150

1. The National Museum of Korea is a small museum. **Yes** **No**
2. There are thousands of things in the museum. **Yes** **No**
3. It has a children's museum. **Yes** **No**
4. It has a room that teaches about old homes in Korea. **Yes** **No**
5. It has old clothing from Korea. **Yes** **No**
6. There is no place to eat at the museum. **Yes** **No**

D Listen. Then read and choose the correct answer. 🔊 151

1. Where does Yuki go every day at 8:00?

a.    b.    c.

2. Where does Jack like to go on the weekend?

a.    b.    c.

3. What is Etta's favorite place?

a.    b.    c.

E Complete the missing words.

1. I can meet you at your h_____ after school.

2. What's your favorite food at this r_____

3. My class visited an art m_____ last month.

4. I can walk to my s_____ from my home.

Speak

Circle the action words in the sentences. Then think of your own sentences with action words. Tell your partner.

Turn right on Main Street.

Walk straight down the street.

> **Remember!**
> Use action words to tell people where to go and what to do.

Listen

LISTENING GOAL:
Listen for Setting

Remember!
The **setting** is *where* and *when* something happens.

A Listen to the story **Too Busy!** What do you hear about?
Choose ✔ or ✘. 🔊 152

1.

a girl writing
an e-mail ✔ ✘

2.

a girl taking
classes ✔ ✘

B Think about **Too Busy!** Choose ✔ or ✘.

1. Jan is at home in the story. ✔ ✘

2. In the story, Jan goes to art class,
    swimming class, and a music lesson. ✔ ✘

3. Her classes are on Tuesday morning. ✔ ✘

C Listen to **Too Busy!** again. Choose the correct answer. 🔊 153

1. Where is Jan on Monday afternoon?
    ☐ a. school   ☐ b. town center   ☐ c. home

2. What class does she have first?
    ☐ a. music lesson   ☐ b. swimming class   ☐ c. art class

3. How long does Jan have between her swimming class and
    her music lesson?
    ☐ a. five minutes   ☐ b. ten minutes   ☐ c. an hour

4. What is Jan wearing at the end of the story?
    ☐ a. a coat   ☐ b. a baseball cap   ☐ c. her swimsuit

D Listen and write the word. Then choose the correct picture. 🔊 154

1. _____

☐ a.   ☐ b.

2. _____

☐ a.   ☐ b.

3. _____

☐ a.   ☐ b.

4. _____

☐ a.   ☐ b.

E Complete the sentences.

go to swimming class	see a play	take an art class
have a music lesson	write an e-mail	practice violin

1. I _____ to my grandmother in Mexico every week.

2. I _____ in music class. I am getting very good!

3. Do you want to _____ with me at the new theater?

4. We like painting so we _____ after school.

F Unscramble and write.

1. e p c r i a t c   i v l o n i

_____

2. v e a h   a   s u c i m   s e o s n l

_____

3. e s e   a   y l a p

_____

4. i r e t w   n a   i m l a e

_____

Listen

LISTENING GOAL:
Listen for Descriptions

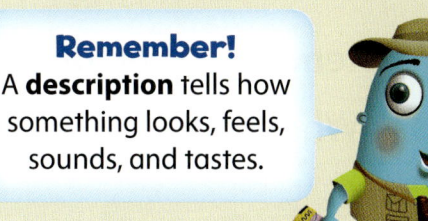

Remember!
A **description** tells how something looks, feels, sounds, and tastes.

A Listen to the article **Go to Sleep!** Then put the pictures in order. 155

A

B

C

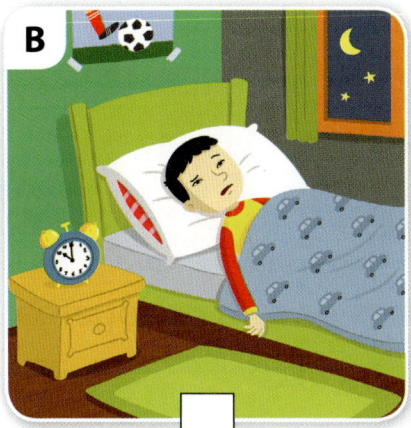

B Think about **Go to Sleep!** How are different things described in the article? Choose ✔ or ✗.

1. The weather is warm. ✔ ✗

2. The music is strange. ✔ ✗

3. The nap is long. ✔ ✗

C Listen to **Go to Sleep!** again. Choose **Yes** or **No**. 156

1. It is always easy to fall asleep.   **Yes**   **No**

2. There is nothing you can do to help.   **Yes**   **No**

3. It can help to go for a walk.   **Yes**   **No**

4. It can help to get exercise.   **Yes**   **No**

5. Be quiet before you go to sleep.   **Yes**   **No**

6. Listen to loud music.   **Yes**   **No**

D Listen. Then read and choose the correct answer. 🔊 157

1. What does Dan want?

a.  b.  c.

2. What does the girl want?

a.  b.  c.

3. What do the children always do together?

a.  b.  c.

E Complete the missing words.

1. We often g_____ in the park.

2. I like to l_____ before I go to sleep.

3. Let's m_____ car together.

4. Let's stay home this afternoon and p_____

Speak

**Circle the description words in the sentences.
Then think of your own sentence with description words.
Tell your partner.**

I like to listen to loud music in the morning.

The math homework is hard.

Listen

LISTENING GOAL:
Listen for What Is Similar

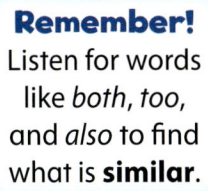

A Listen to the story **Who Is Happy?** What do you hear about? Choose ✔ or ✘. 🔊 158

1.

two boys   ✔ ✘

2.

two girls   ✔ ✘

B Think about **Who Is Happy?** What is similar about the two people? Choose ✔ or ✘.

1. They are both 10 years old.   ✔ ✘

2. They both are sons of kings.   ✔ ✘

3. They are both happy.   ✔ ✘

C Listen to **Who Is Happy?** again. Choose the correct answer. 🔊 159

1. How does James feel?
   ☐ a. happy   ☐ b. unhappy   ☐ c. tired

2. Whose hair does Ben brush?
   ☐ a. James' hair   ☐ b. his hair   ☐ c. his sister's hair

3. What is in Ben's garden?
   ☐ a. fruits and vegetables   ☐ b. flowers   ☐ c. only fruits

4. Who takes care of Ben's garden?
   ☐ a. Ben   ☐ b. Ben's sister   ☐ c. James

D Listen and write the word. Then choose the correct picture. 🔊 160

1. _____

☐ a.   ☐ b.

2. _____

☐ a.   ☐ b.

3. _____

☐ a.   ☐ b.

4. _____

☐ a.   ☐ b.

E Complete the sentences.

| garden   comb   mirror   sink   brush   stairs |

1. You look in the _____ too much!

2. I walk up lots of _____ to get to this class.

3. This _____ has many beautiful flowers.

4. You can get water at the _____

F Unscramble and write.

1. m o b c

_____

2. u h r s b

_____

3. s i a r t s

_____

4. k i n s

_____

Listen

LISTENING GOAL:
Listen for What Is Different

A Listen to the article **Rugs**. Then put the pictures in order. 🔊 161

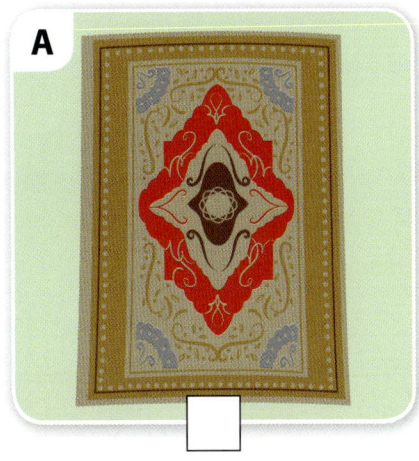

A

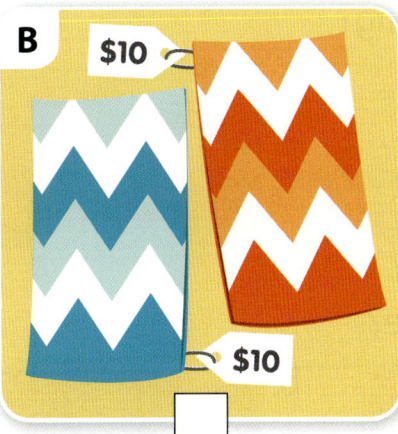

B
$10
$10

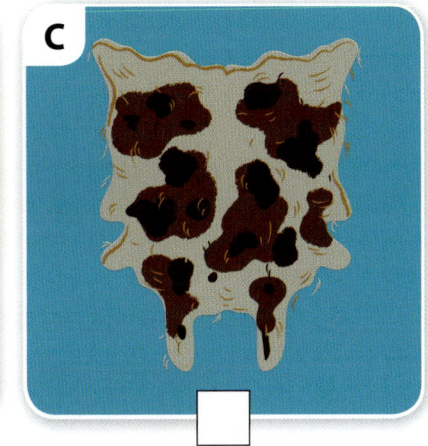

C

B Think about **Rugs**. What things are different now than they were before? Choose ✔ or ✗.

1. Rugs were hard to make, but now they are not.　✔　✗

2. People used rugs, but now they do not use rugs.　✔　✗

3. Rugs were only in rich people's homes, but now
   they are in many homes.　✔　✗

C Listen to **Rugs** again. Choose Yes or No. 🔊 162

1. First, people used parts of trees and grass to make rugs.　**Yes**　**No**
2. First, people used rocks to make rugs.　**Yes**　**No**
3. The rugs we know today started in the United States.　**Yes**　**No**
4. Some of the rugs we know today started in Egypt.　**Yes**　**No**
5. The rugs we know today started about 2,500 years
   before now.　**Yes**　**No**
6. Today, rugs are not hard to make.　**Yes**　**No**

D Listen. Then read and choose the correct answer. 🔊 163

1. What is the boy looking for?

a.    b.    c.

2. Where is Beth sitting?

a.    b.    c.

3. What does she like?

a.    b. 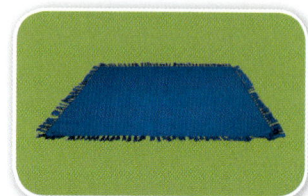   c.

E Complete the missing words.

1. I'm making a cake in the o_____

2. My sister is sleeping on the s_____

3. The b_____ is in this bathroom.

4. The milk is in the r_____

> **Remember!**
> To make a comparison, use phrases like *as well*, *similarly*, and *on the other hand*.

Speak

Circle the phrases *as well*, *similarly*, or *on the other hand* in the sentences. Then think of your own sentences and make comparisons. Tell your partner.

I live in an apartment, and my best friend does as well.

My home is near school. On the other hand, it is far from town.

Picture Dictionary

Write the key words.

Unit 1

_____

_____

_____

_____

_____

_____

Unit 2

_____

_____

_____

_____

_____

_____

Unit 3

_____

_____

_____

_____

_____

_____

Unit 4

_____

_____

_____

_____

_____

_____

Picture Dictionary

Unit 5

_____

_____

_____

_____

_____

_____

Unit 6

_____

_____

_____

_____

_____

_____

Unit 7

_____

_____

_____

_____

_____

_____

Unit 8

_____

_____

_____

_____

_____

_____

Unit 9

_____

_____

_____

_____

_____

_____

Unit 10

_____

_____

_____

_____

_____

_____

Unit 11

_____

_____

_____

_____

_____

_____

Unit 12

_____

_____

_____

_____

_____

_____

Syllabus

Topic	Unit	Listening Goal	Key Words	Speaking Goal
TOPIC 1 The Working World	Unit 1	Listen and take notes	*driver, judge, musician, news reporter, scientist, tailor*	Ask and give personal information
	Unit 2	Listen for the 5 Ws	*astronaut, author, cashier, engineer, mechanic, singer*	Focus: The 5 Ws
TOPIC 2 In My Backpack	Unit 3	Listen for facts	*calculator, dictionary, folder, scissors, stapler, workbook*	Agree and disagree
	Unit 4	Listen for opinions	*cabinet, drawer flag, laptop, shelf, tablet*	Focus: Phrases for agreeing and disagreeing
TOPIC 3 I Like Your Clothes	Unit 5	Listen for preferences	*baseball cap, coat, handbag, shorts, sneakers, swimsuit*	Give preferences
	Unit 6	Listen for reasons	*clean, dirty, heavy, light, thick, thin*	Focus: Phrases for giving preferences
TOPIC 4 All Around Town	Unit 7	Listen for sequence	*airport, bank, home, playground, post office, zoo*	Ask for and give directions
	Unit 8	Listen for directions	*amusement park, apartment, bookstore, museum, restaurant, school*	Focus: Action words for directions
TOPIC 5 Busy, Busy, Busy!	Unit 9	Listen for setting	*go to swim class, have a music lesson, practice violin, see a play, take an art class, write an e-mail*	Give a description
	Unit 10	Listen for descriptions	*go for a walk, have fun, listen to music, make a model, play a board game, take a nap*	Focus: Description words
TOPIC 6 Home Sweet Home	Unit 11	Listen for what is similar	*brush, comb, garden, mirror, sink, stairs*	Make a comparison
	Unit 12	Listen for what is different	*armchair, bathtub, oven, refrigerator, rug, sofa*	Focus: Phrases for making comparisons